D1586155

Published in 2009 by
Laurence King Publishing Ltd
361–373 City Road
London EC1V 1LR
United Kingdom
T +44 20 7841 6900
F +44 20 7841 6910
E enquiries@laurenceking.com
www.laurenceking.com

This book was produced by
Laurence King Publishing Ltd, London.

A catalogue record for this book is
available from the British Library.

ISBN (hardback): 978 1 85669 665 4
ISBN (paperback): 978 1 85669 626 5

Designed by Untitled

Printed in China

CREATIVE ISLAND II
INSPIRED DESIGN FROM GREAT BRITAIN
JOHN SORRELL

Acknowledgements

Producing this book has been a team effort and I would like to pay tribute to the brilliant work of my colleagues. Adriana Paice has played a key role as curator, editor and co-ordinator – the book would not have happened without her. Nick Skeens has carried out long and sometimes complex interviews and somehow edited them to work in context. Glenn Howard at Untitled has designed the book with great skill and patience. Mary-Jane Gibson's picture research has resulted in some stunning images. It has been a pleasure to work with these great people and all my other colleagues and contributors.

CREATIVE ISLAND II

John Sorrell: This is the second edition of *Creative Island*, a celebration of the inspired design that has come out of Great Britain during the first ten years of the new millennium. The works featured in this book, by designers, architects, artists and engineers, are just some examples of the extraordinary creativity that has emerged from within these shores. But, I should add, this is not just about British designers working for British clients – many are from overseas but have chosen to base their practice here, and some of their work has found its final, physical, form across the globe, from Hollywood to Shanghai.

So why is this such a creative island? The UK continues to be seen as one of the leading nations in design. We may be an island people but there is nothing insular about the way design works here; practitioners study each other's work, meet socially and interact at industry events and forums. This leads to a healthy sense of competition as well as to mutual learning, development and innovation. And all this is fostered by a forward-thinking design education system that encourages cross-fertilisation and collaboration across the disciplines. Our universities and colleges continue to thrive and to attract students from all over the world – many of whom decide to stay and join what some have called a multicultural hotbed of design thinking.

I'm very interested in how creative people generate their ideas. You can take completely different design disciplines that work on opposite scales – say, architecture and jewellery design – and, with a little examination, recognise the same creative thought processes. Designers often employ the same type of thinking no matter what they are working on.

We have interviewed more than 100 different designers about their work and the way in which they come up with their ideas. Sebastian Conran talks about how he walked on Chesil Beach and found inspiration for his Equilibrium Scales among the pebbles. Terence Woodgate describes how at a social function he became jealous of Formula One's access to exotic materials and so collaborated with John Barnard to create an amazing table. Christopher Kane says he often starts from "the opposite direction", working with ugliness to gain inspiration. Simon Heijdens explains how his focus on the randomness of nature in his light installations grew out of the "rigidly defined" Netherlands environment of his youth. And Norman Foster says he thinks the creative process is all about listening and then asking the right questions.

In many of the interviews, designers confess their influences and talk about experimentation, inspiration, sense of humour and, perhaps most important of all, how their best work so often comes from close and collaborative relationships with their clients.

At the heart of this book is an exploration of 26 different design disciplines, from engineering and architecture at one end to textiles and jewellery at the other, with so many in between. I've divided the book into ten themes, the last of which is *Projections*, which takes a look at projects yet to be realised.

Reflections is about developing new ideas from the heritage of design tradition, such as Ozwald Boateng's Savile Row suits or Martin Lambie-Nairn's redesign for the BBC on-screen identity. *Renewal* is about regenerating existing designs, such as Mark Porter and Paul Barnes's recreation of *The Guardian*, or Alastair Lansley's redesign of St Pancras station. *Subversion* is all about design that makes you do a double-take, such as Jake Phipps's Jeeves and Wooster lightshades or Simon Waterfall's radical clothes designs under the brand name "Social Suicide". *Humanism* is about putting human experience at the centre of design, such as Steve Harding-Hill's reworking of Aardman's *Creature Comforts* to highlight the challenges of disability, or James Dyson's reinvention of the hand dryer. *Transformation* describes design that seems to evolve in front of your eyes, such as Hussein Chalayan's motion dresses or Thomas Heatherwick's Rolling Bridge. *Fluidity* is about the grace and beauty of curvature and flow: Jacqueline Durran's design for Keira Knightley's green dress in the film *Atonement* or Ross Lovegrove's Ty Nant water bottle are just two examples. *Precision* is about pinpoint accuracy, such as Doug McKiernan's work on McLaren's 2007 Formula One car and Angus Hyland's book *Marks* for Pentagram. *Transparency* is about design that celebrates translucence, such as Richard Rogers's Welsh Assembly and Marc Newson's Atmos clock. *Monumentality* is about design that feels massive and bold, from Alan Kitching's typography for a book about the Royal Albert Hall to Amanda Levete's Selfridges store in Birmingham.

Design is the engine room of the creative industries, not just here but everywhere. It seems to me that every major nation in the world is trying to find ways to harness the creativity of its people. Why? Because creativity is what sets the human race apart, enabling us to solve the problems we face and make a better world for us all to live in. Perhaps it has never been so important to get more people thinking creatively. *Creative Island*, then, is about creative thought and brilliant design, and how they come to be.

FLUIDITY

124
liquescence, liquefaction, flux, fusion, wetness, deliquescence, thaw, molten, runny, flow, curvaceous

PRECISION

146
accurate, truthful, exact, meticulous, rigorous, finite, hi-fidelity, dead-on, unerring, punctual, right, infallible, fastidious, fair dinkum

TRANSPARENCY

170
translucent, hyaline, crystalline, see-through, pellucid, transpicuous, diaphanous, revealing, naked, sheer, nude, exposed, honest

MONUMENTALITY

192
symbol, myth, statement, big, enormous, grand, great, vast, gigantic, immense, magnificent, majestic, spacious, mighty, eminent, abundant

PROJECTIONS

212
prediction, casting, forecasting, overhang, jut, forewarning, prophecy, prognosis, foresight, prospectus, prospect, protrusion, future projects

REFLECTIONS

EMBLETON BAY, NORTHUMBERLAND, ENGLAND

This chapter is all about drawing on heritage, tradition and great work from the past to create new things. For Becky Oldfield at Lost and Found Design this process began as a visit to the market.

Rebecca Oldfield: About five years ago I was picking my way through Greenwich market when I came across an old naval flag. It was damaged but still beautiful, and so cleverly made. My background is textiles; I had some sewing and darning skills so I bought the flag and started repairing it. That sparked off the collector in me. I became fascinated by Coronation flags, which are made each time we have a new monarch. If you compare a 1953 Queen Elizabeth II flag to the equivalent for Queen Victoria in 1838, the difference in quality and style is enormous. A hundred years ago they put a lot more effort into the flags, more colours, more intricacy, more strength, more stitching; they're built to last. A brand-new flag is all very well, but much more interesting is one that has hung over cub-scout gatherings for 50 years in an old village hall, or has thrashed its hem out in a mid-Atlantic gale aboard a Royal Navy destroyer. That's how this product line began.

It's all about making new products from historical stuff, saving it from rotting away in the bottom drawer. I'm recycling heritage that might otherwise never be seen, giving old things new life. To me that's more interesting than making or buying something completely new. I began making the flags into cushions, embellishing them with military paraphernalia, like old naval buttons embossed and made from solid brass.

If a flag is really damaged, I'll cut it up and piece it together, using army-issue thread and traditional buttonhole techniques. It's the attention to detail that's really important.

The Jubilee lamp (pictured) is made up from an entire flag that's been hand-stitched and twisted over a vintage frame. The flag was in good condition, so, if you wanted, you could unpick it to celebrate a British sports victory or signal distress… I try not to damage them. The braiding is antique and the buttons come from a Second World War uniform. It's lined with white muslin and glows nicely. Some of the pieces are meant to have a sense of humour, to wink at times past.

I'm learning about our history all the time and it's opened up a whole new area for me. People are very proud of their history. A former army officer gave me his own flag and presented me with a lot of his personal memorabilia that had just been sitting in a box. I repaired his old campaign camp bed with his flag, and decorated it with regimental ribbons and stripes from his uniform. Now it's a conversation piece, something he can look at every day, a desirable object of personal worth that he can use. It would be great if things like this were passed down to future generations.

Another successful line has been the deckchairs, made with flags buttoned on to the frames. Sometimes I make four deckchairs out of a large Union flag, so that, when you put the deckchairs together, the flag is reassembled. People say the deckchairs make them smile. They've become so much in demand that I now do a screen-printed version with new flags made from organic fabric, distressed to look old. But they are still buttoned with original military buttons.

JUBILEE LAMP

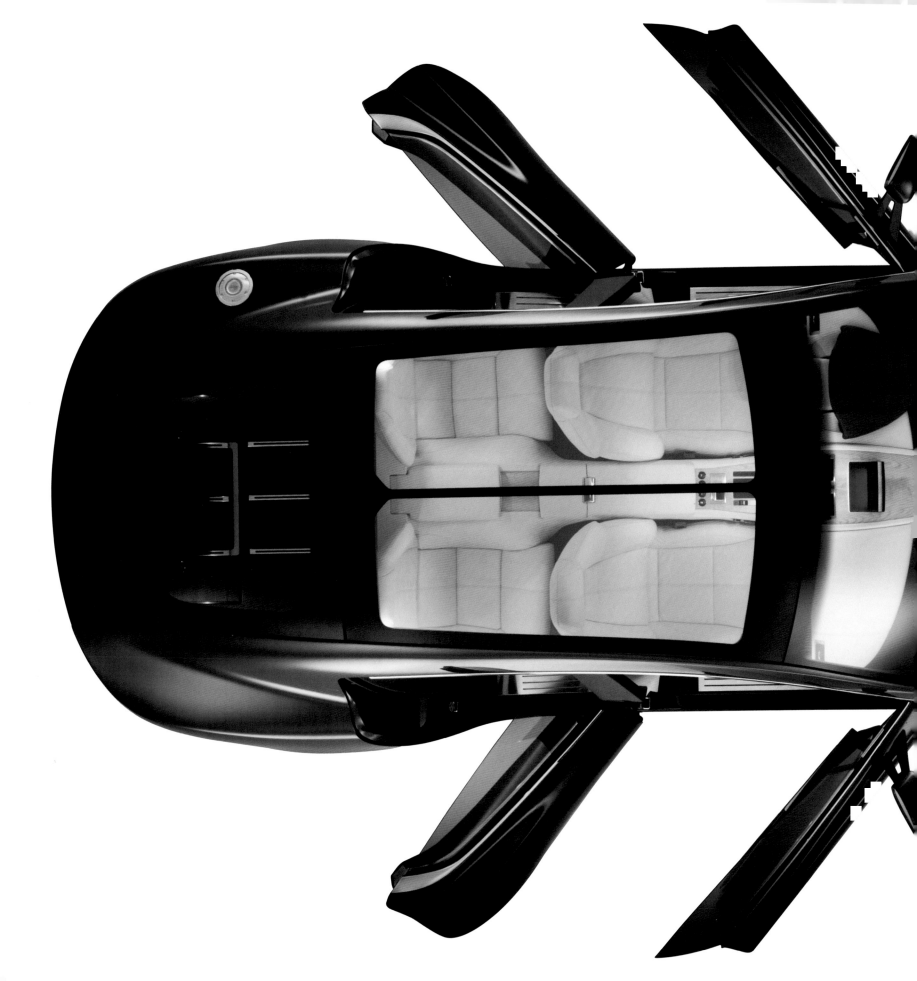

When I asked Marek Reichman which Aston Martin he would like to see in this book, he replied, without hesitation: "The Rapide – it was the biggest challenge to design." The heart of that challenge was to create a classic Aston Martin sports car – with four doors.

Marek Reichman: My brief was simply expressed: "Please design for Aston Martin the most beautiful four-door sports car in the world." The aim was to give people the cachet of having a dynamic sports car that you can really share – you can take your friends on a trip down to the South of France in a Rapide.

It's our most elegant expression of the Aston Martin, and that's been made possible by its longer wheelbase. The extra length and width has allowed us to create more flow and better proportions. We had in mind the image of a silk scarf blowing in the wind. It may not be so beautiful if you crumple it, but if you let it flow, you get these incredible lines and shapes.

A lot of credit has to go to the incredible skills of the clay modellers. This is not a computer-designed car – all the concepts were done in ballpoint pen and clay. And the initial shape came very quickly. I sketched the car as I saw it, and gave the sketch to the clay modelling team, who built a model based on the sketch that was some 40 per cent the size of the real one. We began work in 2005, when we actually had a summer. That meant we could view the model outside – it's always best to set the models against the infinity perspective of the sky. It was just *right*; spot on, straight away.

I was encouraging the team to think of a racehorse at speed with the sinews stretched… The modellers have a superb understanding of how you can make a shape feel lithe and athletic rather than heavy and muscle-bound. By working to refine every surface, to make the light fall on it just so, the modelling team managed to make the Rapide present a graceful stance from every angle. They work with immense passion and dedication.

Designing the Rapide has been a pretty emotive process; inevitable really, because we are trying to generate an emotional response. We want people to see the dynamism of the car whether it's parked by the village green or flashing down the Autobahn. We want people to see it and just go: "Wow! That's beautiful!"

And of course, it's packed out with all the latest luxuries. SatNav (of course), a full I-CE system (In-Car Entertainment), DVD screens in the headrests, iPod connections, and headphones if you don't want to share your film or music with other people in the cabin.

It's the most flexible car we've ever designed. The boot is open-plan with no bulkheads, adding to the sense of space, which is further amplified by the transparent, panoramic, polycarbonate roof. The boot also features power points for an optional fridge; or, if you prefer, you can put in a lockable gun chest for clay-pigeon shooting.

And, of course, the interior is leather throughout; we're using a shagreen leather, which has a soft snakeskin feel. The doors open with the same "swan-wing" motion of the DB9. The powerhouse is the DB9's V12 engine, with horsepower peaking at 480. And, in a first for Aston Martin, the brakes and calipers are made of carbon.

We first unveiled it, to considerable acclaim, in 2006 at the Detroit motor show. It should be on sale in the third quarter of 2010.

ASTON MARTIN RAPIDE

David Pearson was fresh out of college when, by chance, he got the opportunity of a lifetime, and took it with both hands.

David Pearson: This all arose out of me panicking at college about what I was going to do afterwards. I was studying graphic design, specialising in typography, and I knew a whole bunch of us would be spat out of Central St Martins at the same time. So I started to apply for jobs well before I graduated, and got one as a junior text designer at Penguin. I started the day I left college.

Six months later I was made redundant. But at the last minute I was asked to stay on and work in the cover design department. Most designers in that department understandably want to work with modern-day, living authors. So when commissioning editor Simon Winder came up with the idea of trying to push sales of the classics by using a pamphlet format, no one was biting his hand off for the task. And, as there were no sales expectations, they passed it onto a junior. Which was me.

It was a very lucky break and I was given a very free hand. I had no images foisted on me, no agent to liaise with, no estate insisting on x or y. So, as a trained typographer, I decided just to use text to create a feel that was somehow contemporary to the writer.

To my mind, that meant dropping the Penguin logo from the cover – which was a pretty bold step for a junior! So you'll not be surprised to hear I hid my work from Penguin until it was finished, doing most of my work quietly up at St Bride Printing Library.

I created some parameters around the red and black colour palette, and I got other designers involved: Phil Baines, my tutor and mentor from Central, plus Catherine Dixon and Alistair Hall. Phil did five and I did about 13 of the first 20 covers; this gave the series a good sense of pace and variety. Phil was far more confident in his use of space: he did Marcus Aurelius's *Meditations* cover, breaking all the rules by breaking up the author's name and the book title! I tended to be a little more constrained and ornate.

It was obvious Penguin didn't have huge expectations, so when I finally presented the ideas they were pleasantly surprised. They found themselves judging an entire aesthetic, rather than just the covers.

The series has done extremely well. Copies of, say, George Orwell, in the standard Penguin edition, might sell a few thousand a year – but in the new pamphlet edition it was selling something like 200,000.

It took a very trusting publisher to give me that freedom. I doubt I'll ever get it again!

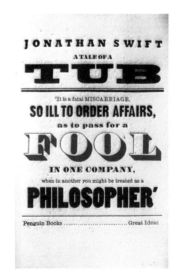
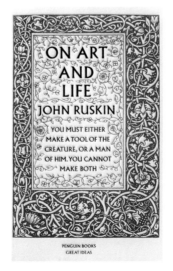
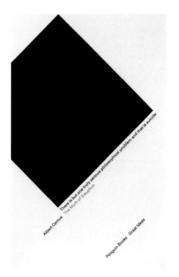

MARCUS AURELIUS · MEDITATIONS · A LITTLE FLESH, A LITTLE BREATH, AND A REASON TO RULE ALL — THAT IS MYSELF

PENGUIN BOOKS

GREAT IDEAS

I've followed Ozwald Boateng's career with great interest and watched him develop to the point where he now has a shop in a prime position on Savile Row – the heart of traditional English tailoring. Ozwald continues those traditions but has evolved a unique approach that combines creativity with spirituality.

Ozwald Boateng: If you're looking to define what I do, it's in the cut. I have a particular way of cutting that creates a formality and harks back to the past traditions. I then use modern details to make the traditional look contemporary. For example, I pay a lot of attention to pockets – where they're positioned, how they are slanted – and I take a similar approach to buttons. A traditional birdseye fabric comes in a black or a grey – I translate that into a modern colour: a purple or a tonic blue. Over 20 years I've created millions of fabrics – each time I design a cloth I create a series of colour waves through the warp and the weft, offering hundreds of options. The real skill in design is to trust your instinct and dovetail that into your work. I base all of my creativity on the way I feel; I guide myself through my own instincts when I create.

Every designer is evolving; when I started it was all about taking tradition and making it modern to inspire young people to want to be a part of it; that was the drive for me. And I knew that by mixing this concept I could revolutionise the traditional viewpoint and inspire tailors and menswear designers to look at themselves more as couturiers; creative opportunities for couturiers are greater than those for tailors.

Clients have said that my suits bring the best out of them, building not only their confidence, but a belief in themselves. So now I've opened a new store on Savile Row to reflect how my creativity has become more closely linked to my spirituality. I've tried to make the shop more of a spiritual home for men's luxury, where you can be with yourself and find yourself: more about inward knowledge than outward display.

When you come into the shop, you automatically slow down. The suits hang in cupboards, and, unless you are directly in front of them, you can't see them. It forces you to walk in a slow manner, like you're moving from painting to painting in an art gallery. The stock sits behind a door beyond the display suit, and that makes it much easier to access. Quick accessibility is important because men are so impatient! I've ensured that the changing rooms are soundproofed, so you can be left alone with your suit and have some time completely to yourself. The whole idea is about getting people more in tune. It's a very conscious philosophy. Before, my work was about redefining tradition; now it's all about helping people get in tune with their spirit. I've always trusted what I feel: that's where I've arrived at – my spirit and my creativity are one, and I feel more confident than ever.

OZWALD BOATENG SAVILE ROW

Smythson, renowned for more than a century for its innovative range of leather accessories, diaries and bespoke stationery, wanted to update its ready-to-write stationery. So creative director Samantha Cameron turned to fashion designer Giles Deacon to help. It was an inspired choice.

Samantha Cameron: We've wanted to use line drawings on our correspondence stationery for a while but have been waiting to find the right illustrative style – certain lines reproduce better than others with our die-stamped engraving techniques. We saw Giles's illustrations in *Vogue* and were drawn to them immediately. What was really exciting about the project was the juxtaposition of the traditional Smythson engraving and the illustrative techniques used by Giles with the edgy modernity of his dress designs. It embraces what Smythson is about – how we have evolved over the years whilst constantly staying true to our heritage and standards.

Working with Giles was a real pleasure. He submitted his illustrations on the first meeting, then he chose the colours of the tissue linings. We only had to produce one set of samples and they were approved within a month of our first conversation. The fact that we have our own manufacturing in the UK with our printers in Swindon made the whole process much easier to manage.

The reaction from the media and our customers has been phenomenal. There is a revived demand for beautiful stationery in this technological age; people are recognising how thoughtful it is to send a handwritten note through the post as opposed to a hasty text or email. The cards went in-store just after Christmas in January 2009. We sold out in the first week and have been struggling to keep them in stock ever since.

Giles Deacon: I've used Smythson notebooks since graduating from Central St Martins in 1992. The jolly outer colours and the unique featherweight paper always inspire me to get ideas down quickly or to spend time on more complex detailed work, so when Samantha approached me I was both delighted and excited to see where the project would go.

The brief was to provide eight fine line-drawn illustrations that had a feeling of spontaneity yet were recognisable as having the Giles signature of "modern British glamour". The inspiration was a mixture of past season favourites and some yet-to-be-seen designs; a mix of nostalgia and future fantasy. From the eight, Samantha and I between us selected five. Individual colours for the hand-lined tissue were chosen to represent each drawing. My aim was to produce drawings that I hoped were interesting, beautiful and collectable.

The relationship with everyone at Smythson was great. From the first meeting the direction was clear and I knew I was in safe, professional hands. All I had to do was make sure my end worked well. Seeing the first strike-offs reassured me that the quality was everything I had hoped for from such an established and revered company.

To be honest, I don't have a single favourite from the collection; the whole project felt really special. I was really proud of them all.

SMYTHSON

One of my earliest memories is visiting the Festival of Britain in 1951; I remember the Royal Festival Hall as a symbol of bold, modern optimism. But over the intervening years, it's suffered from the ravages of time. Allies and Morrison were appointed to return it to its former glory.

Paul Appleton:
The brief evolved over a number of years and was, essentially, in three parts: to recover the public spaces of the foyers; to retune the auditorium (Simon Rattle famously said that after 20 minutes rehearsing in the Festival Hall you lose the will to live); and to improve the public realm around the building.

In 1963, the front door was moved to the waterfront, which effectively displaced the original circulation through the building. Windows got covered over and the foyer space became increasingly restricted. So we've opened up the foyers again and, by moving the admin offices into a new building between the hall and the railway, we've increased room in the foyer by 30 per cent. That's made it a much more welcoming and generous space, permitting facilities like the ticket office to be accommodated without compromising the building, and allowing visitors to appreciate the original architects' beautifully resolved plan.

The auditorium's original acoustic designers aimed to project sound to the back of the hall while simultaneously softening the echoes from what is, effectively, a concrete box. They were, perhaps, too successful in both these aims – the sound was projected so completely away from the stage and the echo damped so thoroughly that performers sometimes found it hard to hear what they were playing. So we worked with Kirkegaard Associates to alter the geometry of the stage end and to make all the auditorium surfaces more reflective and reverberative. One of the many tools we used to do this was Kirkegaard's 1/20th scale model of the new auditorium – we tested it with music played at a correspondingly adjusted frequency. The consensus is that the new hall shows a marked acoustical improvement.

Outside, we've made the building much more accessible from the waterfront. Previously it was cocooned in walkways and concrete balustrades, so we removed a major walkway, created a generous elevated terrace, replaced concrete balustrades with glass and re-established the building's relationship with the river. The shops and restaurants now face outwards, welcoming people into the building and turning what was a rather dreary outdoor area into something altogether more alive.

This is the change we're most proud of; now the spaces around the Festival Hall really live up to the excitement and vitality within it. It feels like the Festival Hall has engaged with the city, and the city is answering back.

ROYAL FESTIVAL HALL

When the Royal Mail asked Johnson Banks to create a set of Beatles stamps, Michael Johnson combined a completely new idea with the golden rule of stamp design: less is more.

Michael Johnson: The brief asked for a set of stamps showing Beatles merchandise to mark the fiftieth anniversary of Lennon and McCartney's first meeting. Well, as no doubt the Royal Mail expected (we'd worked for them before), we did some merchandise ideas but also went off down a different road.

We thought the album covers would make the best focus for the stamps. We planned to photograph them in a relevant context; so *Sergeant Pepper's* would be on a raggedy heap of other Beatles LPs amid the shagpile of a late '60s psychedelic student pad. It was while one of our placement students was cutting out the albums in Photoshop that it suddenly dawned on me: "Hang on, we don't need to do the background at all! The covers were icons of the era in themselves; they can do all the work." It's a golden rule of stamp design: less is more – so keep taking things out.

I called the client straight away. I said: "What would happen if we had a raggedy edge to the stamps? Say it was completely asymmetric?" I was trying hard not to give the whole idea away.

They came back a few days later saying it might be possible. When the Royal Mail saw the work, they loved it, despite the fact that Paul and Ringo were set to break their "dead person" rule, which declares that you have to be royal or dead to get on a stamp.

The next hurdle came when we presented the artwork across the table at the printers. Everyone looked blankly at each other. Royal Mail stamps have 0.9mm perforations equidistant around the edge; equidistance was not a feature of the designs I was presenting. The printer said he'd have a go, but when he returned a proof, it looked like mice had been having a go instead. I bit the bullet and learnt the arcane art of perforation design.

Choosing the albums was fun. Some we had to have because they were so iconic – like *Sergeant Pepper's*, even though, arguably, it's a bit too busy for a stamp. I lobbied hard for the *White Album* but lost that one… *Help!*, I knew, would make a killer stamp. And most fans agree *Revolver* is the best Beatles album…

They've been the most successful "non-royal" stamps the Royal Mail has ever had, selling in especially large numbers in Japan and the US. It would have been interesting to see if a more straightforward design would have been as popular, but I'm prepared to bet that the Royal Mail looked at less demanding merchandise-based designs before deciding to go with ours.

THE BEATLES STAMPS

GRAPHIC THOUGHT FACILITY EXHIBITION

The Art Institute of Chicago is expanding its collection to include international, contemporary design in a brand-new wing. While the build was going on, design curator Zoë Ryan decided to invite Graphic Thought Facility to put on an exhibition of their work as a taster. Paul Neale shared the job of presenting the agency's most recent work.

Paul Neale: Zoë Ryan came to England to look at number of studios. When she visited us she said she wanted to introduce us to an American audience through an exhibition dedicated to our work; it was quite a compliment! So we decided to do a survey of a number of projects over the last two years. Zoë also asked us to deal with the design of the space; this made sense as we're often involved in producing graphics for institutional environments.

Huw Morgan and I went over to do a site visit. The size of the proposed gallery was the starting point; it was right in the middle of the museum on the lower ground floor and was a long narrow space, about 12 feet wide, which acted as a conduit to one of the lecture theatres. So we started looking for a physical language to present our work, one that, we decided, should work a little against the formality of museum display. We looked around at noticeboards in public spaces, in parks, libraries, in police station foyers – everywhere!

We didn't want to do a pastiche of noticeboards and we were aware that museum showcases tend to be uniform in colour and dimensions because they are often reused. So we started designing showcases in a variety of different heights, widths and depths to line the two long walls of the gallery, each in its own distinctive, strong palette – we wanted to see how far we could go using a variety of colours. We sprayed the cases in coloured lacquers and extended those colours into a range of beautiful German woollen felts that made up the backboards. We designed bespoke mapping pins to hold the work up and collaborated with an aluminium anodiser to colour the case runners, fixtures and fittings. We also asked the Institute to paint the corridor walls black, to further emphasise the colours; this helped make it clear that this was a special exhibition, not just a decorated passageway.

It was a great opportunity for us. Here was a job in which we could use a lot of colour. We can't always do that; it's not always appropriate. It was also good to do a retrospective and come away with a new idea, a new approach to museum display. The reaction in Chicago was very positive and secured a lot of press.

Zoë Ryan: The Art Institute of Chicago collects and exhibits work from across the globe and dating back centuries. It's had an architecture collection since the 1920s; Chicago has a rich architectural history. When Jim Cuno joined the museum as director he wanted to expand the architecture department to include contemporary and international design in new, specially dedicated galleries totalling some 7,500 square feet.

UK design has always been highly inventive. British designers will typically take a conventional brief and apply new, innovative criteria to create a thought-provoking design; they tailor-make design solutions, becoming problem-solvers as well as authors.

Also, the UK today is such a melting pot, and that means British design can draw on very broad references. It also has a rigorous design education system that continues to generate inventive, creative and imaginative practices driven by the idea of clean, functional utility while staying focused on creating socially and culturally relevant work. All those qualities together have put British creativity at the centre of the design world.

I've long been a fan of Graphic Thought Facility: for me, they're among the most important and inventive graphic designers in the world. They generate a broad scope of projects for institutions, corporations and arts organisations. This exhibition gave me an opportunity to investigate their work and place it with the larger fields of design. They have led the movement away from slickly styled graphics towards work in which the hand-made mark is valued. They're always interested in pushing the boundaries of their materials and production methods. Whether designing publications, exhibitions or brand identities, their work ultimately furthers an appreciation and understanding of the richness of our world.

What's the connection between architecture, classic design and the human foot? United Nude has gained an international reputation from exploring it.

Galahad Clark: I set up United Nude as a creative collective with architect Rem D Koolhaas. For us it's about scaling down architecture and furniture design to the more intimate scale of the human body; and, to my mind at least, that's best expressed through making sexy ladies' shoes!

We launched United Nude with the Möbius, based on the sweep and flow of Mies van der Rohe's iconic Barcelona chair. The form was also inspired by the mathematically fascinating Möbius strip, where a single band forms the inside and the outside – in this case, the sole, heel, foot-bed and upper.

Our third shoe was the Eamz, inspired, of course, by Charles and Ray Eames's classic chair. We looked at the way it uses those beautiful feet to support the central leg and thought we could support a human leg in a similar way.

Our creative process is a bit like the way musicians sample tracks and put them together to make new music.

We take pieces of iconic design and sample them. For the Eamz, we had to do a lot of testing and we had to use much stronger materials than are usually found in shoes; aluminium struts are not exactly run-of-the-mill among cobblers! But the rest of the shoe is pretty traditional, though the last (the foot shape) is particularly generous.

They come in leather and soft suede and have all-leather linings. It continues to be a best-seller. The middle of the sole turns out to be a great place to support your foot – it makes for a bit more stability, spring and give than other high heels; the design won several awards for comfort. Some people have dubbed it "the magic heel" because it looks so improbable! Since the Eamz, other shoe designers have adopted the idea into their own shoes.

We are developing the brand with a series of different shoes, and we've been growing the business pretty fast. Our goal is to create specific iconic products that stand the test of time, rather than concentrating on big seasonal fashion ranges. We challenge ourselves to have a story behind each shoe; it helps give us a creative direction.

And we're exploring new materials and techniques. In fact we're using carbon fibre now; our mould-maker used to make America's Cup yachts!

EAMZ SHOE

The Royal Parks Foundation is a young charity set up to raise money for special projects in London's eight Royal Parks. Deckchair Dreams, managed by Clare Bowen, is both a clever and a beautiful fundraising idea.

Clare Bowen:
We were having an internal meeting in our offices in the middle of Hyde Park. The catering manager, Laurent Trenga, looked out of the window down to the deckchairs and said: "Wouldn't the parks just come alive if all those deckchairs had beautiful designs and colours on them?"

We all perked our ears up, and our chief executive, Sara Lom, said she thought it could be a winner. So it was just a question of finding the funding. Deckchair Dreams was the Foundation's first art project, and it took a year to find someone to support it. In the end, Bloomberg stepped up.

We then invited 25 artists to submit a design in the first year. We didn't want only high art; we also wanted art that was really engaging and intriguing to the public.

Since then we've had contributions from painters, writers, architects, chefs, fashion designers and actors: Raymond Briggs, Tracey Emin, Joanna Lumley – to name a few. The picture opposite shows work by designers Edward Barber and Jay Osgerby, and reflects the different shades of green you can find in Hyde Park in the summer. Each year we have a theme, such as Trees and Wildlife, or Rare and Wonderful Things in the Royal Parks... We then auction off the original artwork, together with a signed deckchair, and sell limited editions of the deckchairs on our website. In one year we raised £100,000 for the parks.

We also run a competition to involve schoolchildren. An artist takes them on a tour of their local Royal Park, teaching them what to look out for and how to draw it. The winning designs from each school are made into deckchairs and an autographed one is sold at auction whilst replicas go into the parks alongside the main collection.

The children enjoy coming to the auction, which is always a pretty grand affair. We offered the same opportunity to the Household Cavalry, who loved taking part. Well, after all, we are the *Royal* Parks...

DECKCHAIR DREAMS

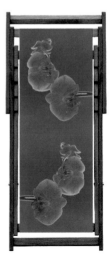

David Mellor's cutlery and tableware are iconic. His son, Corin, carries on the family flair for great design and craftsmanship and has paid tribute to his father by reviving one of his design classics.

Corin Mellor:
The original design was commissioned in around 1963 by the British government. They wanted my father to make a whole series of solid silver pieces for embassies all around the world, including candlesticks, cutlery, teapots and kettles. But the candlesticks fell victim to a round of budget cuts and were only used in the Warsaw and Mexican embassies.

So the originals are very rare. They were handspun in our Park Lane workshop; spinning involves rotating a disc of silver on a lathe and then using a lathe tool to push it over a former to make the hollow base and top. The candlesticks were sold to the government for £120 a pair. To use the same process today would probably cost around £2,000. To make the design accessible to a wider public, we're now making them from solid brass machined with a computer-controlled lathe.

The stem is solid and threaded at each end to take the top and bottom pieces, which are then screwed in and glued with a high-temperature bonding agent before going off to have the brand name laser-etched around the base. When they come back, they are polished, sent for silver plating, and polished again on their return. The look is exactly the same as the originals but, being solid brass, they're much heavier, which is a nice quality. They retail at between £220 and £290.

I have always loved these candlesticks and always thought they should have been revived. It's an incredibly pure piece of design; their shape is so organic that it looks as if they've grown naturally from their bases. The candlesticks have an iconic quality; I can never see them being out of date. They are a simple statement of my father's design genius.

EMBASSY CANDLESTICKS

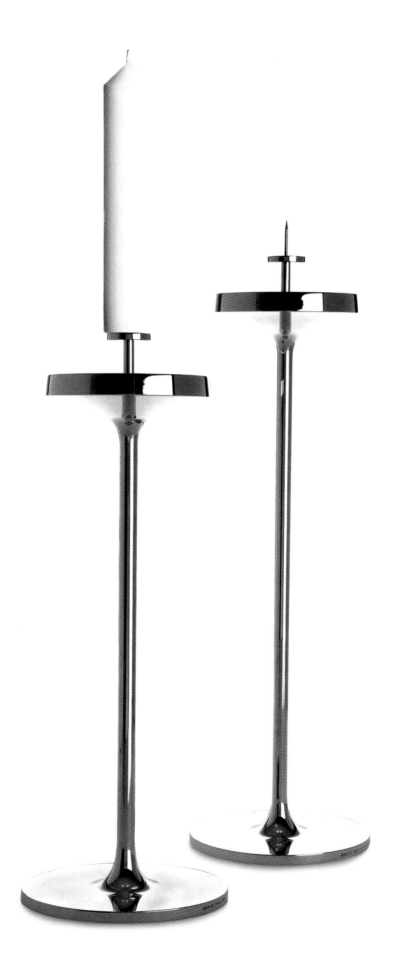

When Martin Lambie-Nairn created a new identity for BBC One, his idea to use a hot-air balloon really caught people's imagination. But it nearly failed to get off the ground.

Martin Lambie-Nairn:

When you face designing something like the BBC One ident, it's a pretty daunting task – like messing with Big Ben or the Union flag. The brief insisted it be modern, confident and inclusive. It also had to create a sense of "oneness", appealing to people from the Shetlands to Land's End.

This project was a real graveyard of good ideas but we finally agreed that the principal tool should be an updated version of the famous BBC spinning globe, used by BBC One since the early '60s. We hit on the idea of creating a sculpture based on the globe, that we could cart round the country, set up, photograph against a local backdrop and then move on, like a circus arriving upon 100 village greens. The BBC liked this idea, but closer study revealed it to be a logistical and financial nightmare.

And then we thought – what about a balloon? They're easy to move over any landscape, they look good on TV – who doesn't love a balloon? It would look great wherever it was, flying over Wimbledon, Cardiff Arms Park... We went for red and yellow, because green and blue, traditional for globes, would have been lost against the sky.

We put the idea before Pam Masters, the BBC head of presentation, who, I can tell you, is no pushover. She loved it. I broke the news that we'd be breaking the £125,000 budget. She said: "Don't worry; for this idea, we'll find the extra."

We took it up to the head of television, Will Wyatt, and he loved it too. But that was not everyone's first response. I remember a crucial meeting attended by all the BBC bigwigs. They kept running the ident on the board-room screen, humming and haaing, drumming their fingers, saying things like, "it's not like any other ident, is it?" or "it's a bit slow – not exactly whizzy." Yes, we nodded, it's calm, confident and beautiful... More tapping of teaspoons. And then, by chance, Will Wyatt wandered in. "Great, isn't it!" he said. They all looked up and nodded: he'd caught them neatly, and luckily, at the tipping point. Good ideas need such serendipity.

BBC ONE IDENTITY

RENEWAL

The renewal of St Pancras Station, a Victorian masterpiece, to house the London terminus for the Eurostar, was an immense task, involving a team made up of architects, engineers and heritage consultants. Alastair Lansley led the architectural team for the final ten years.

Alastair Lansley: The brief was to bring back the grand station to the UK by creating a 21st-century transport interchange that celebrated the best of the past and the present. It included a range of stipulated areas and conditions, including a heritage minimum requirements list. Foster + Partners prepared a master plan that was then developed by LCR's Rail Link Engineering team, a consortium of Bechtel, Arup, Systra and Halcrow.

One of the stipulations was that the renovation of the train shed "had to be as good as Liverpool Street" which caused me to raise an eyebrow, as I had led the redesign there too. I was further influenced by a comment from Norman St John-Stevas (ex-chair of the Royal Fine Art Commission) who was no fan of Liverpool Street, mainly because he felt that the retail, which came later, blocked out the view of the trains. So, from a very early stage, I thought: "The last thing we're going to do is fill the train shed with retail." So St Pancras became an essay in restraint.

St Pancras was originally designed by WH Barlow for the Midland Railway Company after it became clear that neighbouring rival King's Cross Station could not accept more rail traffic from the Midlands. The tracks enter the station 6 metres above the ground having come over Regent's Canal (rather than under it through restricting tunnels, as in the case of King's Cross). If I ever build another station I will bring the tracks in at a similar level; it's so much easier to get under and around the tracks if they come in high, and makes for neater town planning.

The tracks come in at the so-called Barlow Tie, which effectively joined the magnificent curved arches of the train shed to prevent their spreading under the load. Think of the arches as so many bows but imagine that the bowstrings are one-third of the way up the arches, which then curve to the apex in a gentle kiss. Thus the roof support has no visible ties and looks immensely elegant, while a veritable bagatelle of cast-iron columns holds up the train deck which itself forms the Barlow Tie. This is a very efficient design, created in part to provide beer storage beneath the platforms, and fortuitously providing us with a unique opportunity.

St Pancras is Grade 1 listed; as precious to the nation as St Paul's Cathedral. So it was only after painstaking analysis, and approval from English Heritage and London Borough of Camden, that we cut the Barlow Tie to allow light and air down into the undercrop on one side, and escalators and stairways on the other. The undercrop provided the perfect place for retail, allowing us to leave the magnificent shed uncluttered while ensuring the shops are unobtrusive and as polite as Burlington Arcade; certainly not Oxford Street!

The decision presented a major engineering challenge: cutting the tie meant increased lateral pressure on the arches, while the train deck had to support higher loadings from longer trains. The solution was a new 400mm-thick pre-stressed concrete deck independent of the existing grid of wrought-iron beams but supported by bridge bearings on the cast-iron columns. We also extended the train shed to accommodate the new 400-metre-long international trains.

It is an unashamedly modern structure covering all 13 platforms and roofed in glass and aluminium-clad louvre-blades carried some 20 metres above street level on minimal vertical columns, on a large 30-metre grid. The old and the new are separated by a glass transept.

Three new platforms for high-speed domestic services from Kent were built on the east side. It was thus possible to create a new north–south concourse on two levels in the Barlow train shed with the original train deck cut away to link the two spaces.

St Pancras was a massive team effort and was well handled by the government, which was keen to avoid the type of detached arrogance that can lead to conflict and impasse. The legislation insisted on quick consensus: all parties, from English Heritage and London Borough of Camden to a range of railway and historical interest groups, had to work together to resolve all issues. If we couldn't resolve them, then the Secretary of State would. We met nearly every week for five years, and we drew sketches till our hands ached, to explain the ideas and illustrate solutions. I'm delighted to say we never needed the Secretary of State!

The station would have been demolished in the '60s had it not been for Sir Nicolas Pevsner and Sir John Betjeman's inspired campaign; it's why Betjeman's statue, by way of tribute, stands at the top of the stairs and within the glory of the great Barlow train shed.

I'm proud of the simplicity of St Pancras, and the experience it offers. People don't so much walk from the trains as promenade; it's marvellous to watch them look up and around them and take in the beauty of this truly beautiful public space. I think stations like St Pancras help restore the glamour of travel – Europe's destination station. Not many industries can boast such a dramatic rebirth.

ST PANCRAS STATION

Hydrogen fuel cells represent a promising greenhouse-gas-free future for transport and energy production. SeymourPowell has developed a design for a motorbike that could help kick-start the much-needed green revolution.

Nick Talbot: We were approached by the chief executive of the technology company Intelligent Energy. They had developed a fuel cell that pumped out double the power of similar-sized cells and wanted us to come up with a sexy way to demonstrate the technology. The chief executive realised that investors were unlikely to buy into their technology as long as it was a box of wires and tubes sitting on a bench. He wanted people to see it in action and say, "I've got to get into this business!"

We held a top-level creative and strategic session and kicked around a whole load of ideas. Some were about creating a fuel cell that you could bolt on to the side of a house, giving it its own power station. Others included vehicles – a whole range of ideas for different markets. In the end we all plumped for a lightweight vehicle. We decided that some form of scooter would be the way ahead. We chose a bike rather than a small car because a bike needs less fuel and suited the size of the unit better.

Two months later and we'd decided we could create a full-sized prototype motorbike. The aim was to show it could do what it said on the tin – there are a lot of charlatans in this business making daft claims. We designed the bike around the Core, the suitcase-like power unit that lifts out of the heart of the bike and can be carried away by an average person. The fuel cell, the carbon fibre gas bottle and the electronics are all inside the Core. It's a portable power station.

We looked very carefully at the crossover point between a heavy-duty bicycle and a very light motorcycle. Our brief to ourselves was: "Imagine what that hybrid might be." We made the frame out of carbon fibre and thin-walled aluminium tube. Every component was stripped back to be as lightweight as possible. The aerodynamics were not critical: the thing about small motorbikes is that they are dominated by the hulking great block that sits on it – namely, the rider. More of an issue was heat management – the cell produces a lot of heat. Another major concern was safety – the fuel is stored in a high-pressure hydrogen bottle. It's in the centre of the Core, protected from all angles, and is, effectively, armoured.

The early concept sketches resembled an alien artefact more than a bike. We concluded that the eventual market was going to be global, so we didn't want to put people off. We had to find a balance between sexy looks and a practical motorbike. The response has been amazing, with over half a billion hits in terms of press and web; it caught the attention of lots of people. Intelligent Energy have now licensed part of their technology to Suzuki.

The elephant in the room, of course, is filling the bike with fuel. We did a study that showed that if we wanted to kick-start the fuel cell system, we could park a hydrogen fuel truck in locations where the biggest concentration of fuel cell vehicles are expected to be and supply the demand with just one truck and a driver. That looked like the way to get the supply chain going at a low enough cost: you make the filling station as mobile as the customers. To demonstrate this, we took two bikes to an alternative energy electro-vehicle show in Monaco. The organiser had arranged for a German industrial gas company to bring a small hydrogen fuel truck; they parked it up by the superyachts. We rode the bikes from the hotel car park down to the harbour, and filled them up from the back of this vehicle, using the standard nozzle that just about everyone uses in the hydrogen cell business. It was good to show we could bring a bike from another country and just fill her up.

ENV MOTORBIKE

The Westminster Academy at the Naim Dangoor Centre is a design breakthrough for schools. It uses architecture and graphic design to provide the students with a learning environment that is inspiring, creative and corporate – ideal for a school with a business focus. The architects were AHMM and the graphics were done by Studio Myerscough.

Paul Monaghan: Our original sponsor, Nigel Hugill, head of the property developers Chelsfield, gave us a pretty straightforward brief to simply design the "best school in the country". Chelsfield were influential in the decision to make it a business-focused school.

The private sponsorship was taken over by Naim Dangoor, a former Iraqi refugee who was keen to repay the UK for giving his family asylum. Most of the pupils at the school have English as a second language, so internationality and business were two key influences on the design. The architecture celebrates the astonishing fact that the pupils come from over 200 different countries. The welcome sign is in 15 different languages and the café food ranges from falafel to Welsh rarebit – all based on asking the pupils about their favourite foods. The glass screens, which help give the school its sense of space, are marked not with safety dots but with sketches of tall buildings from the world's cities.

We worked very closely with the incoming head teacher, Alison Banks; I was actually part of the team who interviewed her initially for the job; gauging her reactions to one of the early scale models of the school. She was a pioneer in personalised learning and IT and we developed key features with her, including the playgrounds, the branding, internal arrangements and the toilets, which are designed with two exits, so pupils can easily escape any bullies.

We've kept the school's exterior shape simple to maximise the money available for the learning environment; it's simply a low-maintenance colourful skin that uses greens and yellows to contrast with the grey environment (the school is in the shadow of London's Westway dual carriageway). The entire building is clad in glazed terracotta tiles; it's a very special material, colourful from one angle, but from another almost like a mirror. Inside is a complete reversal: we've exposed concrete and timber and used it as a backdrop to the colourful artwork, people, furniture and acoustic panels.

In terms of behaviour, it's all very legible. From certain perspectives you can see right through the whole school. Problem areas like corners and cul-de-sacs have been designed out. Behaviour has been transformed, with bullying reduced to zero and huge improvements in exam results in the first year. The place feels less like a school and more like the HQ of a major international company, which, we think, should make an inspiring learning environment for young business minds.

Morag Myerscough: One of our first jobs was to approach the school "logo"; we had to take into account the fact that it would appear on a huge lightbox at the entrance. It was really important to make it work with the architecture – the physical building was all about strata, so we designed the logo to cut across the strata and go in different directions. You could say it was symbolic of the school preparing its students to move where they wanted in the hierarchical world of business.

The next stage was to work on how to incorporate the school's international business and enterprise theme. Alison Banks, the head teacher, wanted to label the rooms and departments to reflect the educational style. Together we came up with a set of room names that moved away from the traditional classroom names and numbers to names like "break-out space", "green room", "media studies" and "sky dining". We made the room signage big, bold and clear, but there were no directional signs – AHMM's architecture made the school really easy to navigate. The way I work is to do things as simply as possible, so I often prefer to use traditional methods wherever I can, like sign-writing and painting; they appear more human.

This wasn't really a signage project; it was more about creating an environmental graphic narrative that worked alongside the architecture rather than feeling bolted on afterwards. The glazing was a big challenge. We created 16 international cityscapes on the glass partitions showing key buildings in each city, old and new, and their relationship in scale with each other. The brief stressed the need to make the graphics as vandal-proof as possible. Vandalism to signage isn't necessarily conscious – people sometimes absent-mindedly pick at the edges. We did a lot of tests to make sure they couldn't be peeled off.

We had a fantastically responsive client. For the main space, we created a model to show how the big names would work on the balconies. The client took one look at the models and straightaway said Yes! I think the reason why the project flowed really well was that everyone involved tried to take on board all the aspirations of the clients. The amazing thing is that the students haven't spoilt anything. I think when people are given things that others have tried really hard to make as good as possible for them, then they treat the work with respect. So the vandalism that we feared simply hasn't happened.

WESTMINSTER ACADEMY

Snowboarding fashion has become increasingly about individual style and expression. The snowboard manufacturer Burton turned to Paul Smith, who, perhaps more than anyone, is famous for individual flair in clothes design.

Paul Smith: In 2006 Burton asked if we'd be interested in designing a snowboarding jacket that was, to quote them, "very Paul Smith". So I said: "Look, if it's just going to end up looking like a traditional ski jacket, you don't really need me." But they said, "no, you can do what you want", which was wonderful.

So we developed a tweed check with Burton that looked like wool but was, in fact, a three-layer performance fabric ideal against snow, rain and wind. We took a technical yarn and wove it in a traditional way to make the check look really authentic. We pattern-cut a tailored jacket that had a bit more shape and movement in it; each seam was heat-sealed and taped for further waterproofing. We used different traditional horn and corozo nut buttons, with each stitched on with contrasting threads. To go with the jacket we made a double-breasted overcoat in a cavalry twill in exactly the same way.

They also asked me to design a snowboard. I remembered when I was a kid that my father, a photographer, would often ask me to climb up a tree, or balance a bottle on my head for a picture he had in mind – I was his prop. One day I came home to see a white sheet on a washing line, in front of which was an old Persian carpet that he'd wired up to look like it was floating. He said: "Just before you do your homework, sit on this and pretend you're flying." A couple of weeks later he showed me a picture with me soaring among the turrets of the Brighton Pavilion. So when Burton asked me to do the snowboard I thought: "Great – I'll make it like a flying carpet whizzing down a mountain."

SNOWBOARD AND JACKET

Simon Heijdens creates light installations that try to introduce nature's timeline into artificial spaces. His mission is to make people more aware of natural processes within an urban environment.

Simon Heijdens: This started with a commission to do a light project for the city of Eindhoven. More often than not, the decor in human spaces is pretty static, and 24-hour lighting can exclude a sense of connection with the natural day. I grew up in The Netherlands, a highly planned, densely populated, rigidly defined environment. It's probably no surprise that I developed a fascination with the unplanned behaviour of nature. So my idea was to create a site-responsive light installation that had a variable character directly linked to the leftovers of the natural world. In Eindhoven I was trying to trace and amplify natural cycles.

Tree starts at sunset: a tree seems to grow on to the façade of a building as a projection of white light some 8 metres high. It's essentially a drawing built up of hundreds of graphic elements reacting to a wind sensor on top of the building that is being used as a backdrop for the projection. It recreates the exact motion of a real tree if it were to stand in that exact location. The trunk and thicker branches are very stubborn – but the thinner branches and twigs are more sensitive; every part has its own sensitivity to the passing wind. The tree changes throughout the hours and days and seasons. One day it might be static, but on a windy day the branches will be bending and swaying.

In the natural world the ground gives away a lot of information about who has walked there and what the weather's been like, but the urban surface is very much muted. So I try to bring out that narrative and give legibility to the skin of the city, to make it sensitive to the way it's being used. Each time a person passes, a leaf might fall. It's then projected on to the ground nearby the tree. At busy times there will be a high rate of leaf-fall, effectively tracing an image of how the city is being used. The projected leaves are sensitive to human movement, so, as you walk through them, they slowly flutter around your feet, like you're kicking through a pile of leaves. Sometimes they accumulate in alleyways – corners of the city often untouched by art or care – and, because the leaves are made of light, the more they fall, the more the dark alleyway is illuminated.

It's run by software that we developed ourselves, all connected to wind and motion sensors, and the installation is designed to work in demanding outdoor environments. *Tree* has been exhibited around the world, including Rotterdam, Amsterdam, Tokyo, Berlin, New York, Milan, Cologne and Nottingham.

TREE

As the chairman of the London Design Festival, one of my favourite moments was Tom Dixon's "chair grab" in Trafalgar Square, in 2006. A few months later I was in New York and dropped in to see what was new in Moss Design. As I arrived I was amused to see Murray Moss in the middle of installing a copper-coated version of one the chairs in the window. I couldn't believe the coincidence.

Tom Dixon: I've been thinking for some time about how inelegant and old fashioned the modern furniture business is. It's not really globalised; you have to wait ages between concept and delivery to customers, and furniture has to go through a whole gamut of processes, including shipping, warehouses and design shops, before it reaches the clients. This has frustrated me for a long time.

I was examining ways of bypassing retail and the whole logistics chain by going direct to the consumer. I was also inspired by the concept of giving away your core service and making money from other sources, a model that has proved successful for businesses like Google and Hewlett Packard. So all this was born from thinking about what modern furniture services will look like.

I thought one model could be to give away chairs, but have some advertising on them; then the advertising goes direct into homes but the product is given for free. I see the idea of a giveaway as a sort of design democracy, undercutting the elitism of design; it enabled me to do a Robin Hood-type intervention, taking from the rich to give to the poor...

At around this time I was approached by the EPS Packaging Group, which makes expanded polystyrene products. They were keen to show what could be done with their product. They proposed I worked with it for the London Design Festival. I saw a way to marry these ideas to this opportunity: by putting their logo on the chair, I was able to make the chairs completely free. I was also fascinated by the future of manufacturing: the way genetic engineers will be able to grow things on various surfaces. And so evolved the copper-coated chair. This again was about trying to find ways of funding more giveaways. It was a little like Yin and Yang; if I could take this relatively inexpensive chair, coat it in copper and transform it into an expensive, $40,000 chair, then that would pay for more free giveaways.

I was also aware of how polystyrene is used as a sacrificial mould to make jewellery: you put precious metal around the mould and build it up; you effectively grow it, using a modern form of electroplating. To do this with a chair required some new thinking, and, of course, the mould wouldn't be sacrificial – the polystyrene would stay. The scale we were proposing was unheard of and we had to make our own tanks. But it's been worth the effort, and has caused considerable interest. My next public event? I'm giving away free lights in Milan...

Murray Moss: I'm old friends with Tom and we speak regularly. I heard about his installation in Trafalgar Square; it was one of those live performance/product events that Tom enjoys so much and does so well. What I love about this chair is its volume; it's a very big chair, and yet it's so light. Its barrel shape has a rather intricate combination of flat planes and rounded surfaces with deep cavities at the base of the chair – that's very challenging to mould. From a formalistic point of view it's lovely.

Tom (being Tom) was most enthusiastic about an evolution of a design that seemed to be going in the wrong direction, evolving from a mass giveaway to a limited edition art piece. It's more usual for couture to evolve into mass production; I found this reversal really intriguing.

The chair is clothed in an ultra-thin veneer of pure copper. And the best part is that all the properties of the original chair are preserved. So you get a chair in a new skin that is so thin, using a process so technically subtle, that it allows you to see each of the moments in the surface of the polystyrene.

The great thing about the copper is that it patinas so well, and in such a variety of shades. I don't know if Tom predicted this, but it's really lovely. It looks like something that might have been on the seabed for a hundred years! The copper confuses you. You read it as metal and expect it to be cold and industrial. But there's something warm about its proportions and patination. It has a painterly feel, somewhat like Manet. And, of course, when you touch it, it is warm – because the polystyrene beneath is reflecting your body heat and the thin copper conducts the heat very quickly.

It gives you this amazing feeling of the polystyrene actually being heavy metal. It looks tremendously heavy, but go to pick it up and you find it's feather light! It really is full of twists and surprises. The general reaction is fascination. We let them read about it before they touch it, and they love the fact that it's evolved from a family of chairs that was given away in Trafalgar Square; they find the genealogy intriguing. It's a curiosity really, like an 18th-century cabinet of wonders.

CU29 CHAIR

Crawley has a library much loved and much used by its people. Artist Gordon Young and typographer Andy Altmann, a partner in why not associates, worked together on a fresh approach to public signage that involved close consultation with the library's staff and users.

Gordon Young:
It all started with an advertisement drawn to my attention by architects Penoyre and Prasad, who were redesigning the library. As an artist who works in public spaces I thought it looked like an interesting job. I chose to work with Anna Sandberg, who had a track record in public buildings, and Russell Coleman, an artist and an old friend.

I wanted to contrast the architectural "purity" of the place, so I suggested sculptural signage; pillars of green oak resembling a series of totem poles; these wonky, splitting trees would look great amid the clean, new architecture. The idea was inspired by the work of David Nash, whose greenwood sculptures crack and bend. To me these flaws reflect our humanity; the great British public is wonderfully imperfect, with our strange foibles, haircuts and clothes...

Anna put cards in the library books asking, "what's your favourite character, your favourite quote from this book?" We got hundreds of replies. Gradually ideas emerged for quotations to illustrate the library's various sections. That's when we began working with Andy Altmann on the typography.

I was in the library a few weeks ago. I loved seeing this "rustic" imperfection against the perfect architectural environment. The pillars are a long way from the usual public signage and information. I thought, for a modest intervention, it punched above its weight. We'd like to do something like this again; I don't think we've finished mining this particular seam...

Andy Altmann:
We'd all discuss what fonts would work best with different types of books. Some of the type has no obvious graphic relationship with the subject; it was what felt interesting and looked good. It was always a bit of an experiment. What looked good on a computer screen sometimes just didn't work when we sandblasted it into the trunks.

It was good to work with green wood, though it did throw up some problems. As it dried out, it would shrink and crack and the type would become disjoined; sometimes it was too much and we'd have to change the font. But generally the cracks worked to make the type more beautiful. To our surprise we found we could use much smaller letters than we expected. On granite you can safely go down to 30mm letters, but we found 20mm would work on the wood; even the serifs stayed sharp.

We came up with an English Gothic font for *Dracula* in the horror section that looked really great on a tree, with its big curves and strange serifs... We illustrated science fiction with an extract from Terry Pratchett's *Guards! Guards!* using Gridnik, designed in the '60s by Wim Crouwel; it has that inhuman, computer feel. For Jean-Paul Sartre we used handwritten fonts that looked as if someone had scored it on a tree in a park; it felt eerie and counter-intuitive.

For *Through the Looking Glass* we had the whole "cabbages and kings" passage by the Walrus and we tried to fill the whole tree with type using Gill Sans Light in capitals with dashes separating the words. We used Robert Louis Stevenson's *Treasure Island* to illustrate the sound library, using a passage that included the parrot repeating "pieces of eight". We separated the words with Xs, to "mark the spot" where treasure was buried.

It was about getting people involved; to read some of the texts you have to walk round and round the pillar; others require you to cock your head...

CRAWLEY LIBRARY

The story of the East Beach Café is truly extraordinary. Businesswoman Jane Wood was determined to replace a potential local eyesore with a beautiful building that would be loved by the local community and be good for business. She chose Heatherwick Studio to realise her dream.

Jane Wood: I bought a property at auction that faced out to the sea at Littlehampton; nobody had bid for it. On the beach, in front of my new property, was a burger kiosk. Two months later I discovered the owner had permission for a 96-seater burger restaurant! The proposed design was a bit of a monstrosity. I thought – if that gets built, it will spoil the beach for ever.

So, I decided to buy the burger business. Having done so, I also decided to run it for six months, and soon saw it was viable. So now it was time to improve the proposed design. I spoke to several designers but I liked Thomas Heatherwick's approach to the brief the best. He said that the building should belong to the beach not to the architecture behind, which is too varied and too far from the beach to be relevant. He said that the most important thing was the prospect, the view of the sea. And he said it should provide refuge: he likened it to being in a Wendy house in a children's playground; you could see out while feeling safe and cosy inside it.

The local Planning Authority loved the new design; the previous one had received hundreds of complaints, but the beach did need a bigger facility. Thomas's design got no objections.

It's a great building to work in and it's a wonderful place. People love it. The maintenance is cheap – we just oil the metal. It's energy efficient, being sprayed with insulation foam on the inside. But for me, one great bonus is what it says about design. It tells small business people that you don't have to be a corporation to commission great design; because great design makes economic sense. Ours has been a great commercial success; people keep coming back, even in the winter. I see it as a sculpture that happens to be a building.

I think gradually, the Brits are beginning to reinvent the seaside, and, increasingly, there's tremendous opportunity on the seafronts of Britain.

Thomas Heatherwick:
As a client Jane was extraordinary. She took on this kiosk, jumped in and ran it with her daughter, Sophie; she was there, frying the chips and then selling them in plastic sandcastle buckets so children would have something to play with on the beach. When people came in, she'd show them a picture of the proposed design and turn them into vocal supporters and enthusiasts. The result was that the project *only* received letters of support at the planning hearing – more of a testament to her than to us.

The company that made our Rolling Bridge project in Paddington, Littlehampton Welding, is run by Bill Tustin, a real enthusiast for building special projects. We got on so well while working on the bridge that when this project came up in Littlehampton, I knew we had to work with him. There was very little money available – it all had to be paid for by cakes, coffee, buckets of chips and Mr Whippy ice creams…

The design evolved because we needed it to be tough, able to cope with wet children dragging in buckets and spades. But it also needed to polish up nicely for an evening meal.

The site was very long and thin, which meant that we could fill one side with glass so people could look out at the view, but the glass needed protecting: almost 40 metres of it. We knew we needed roller shutters, and this constraint led to the idea of making the entire building out of roller shutter boxes. We used their dimensions to define the relief of the roof and the walls. We staggered the heights because we wanted the dining area to be higher than the kitchen and the toilets.

But there was another influence. The tyranny of much architecture is the "in keeping" question – how much are you in keeping with your surroundings? But our site was on the beach, so the argument went that it should be in keeping with the sea rather than the more distant buildings.

My most powerful impressions of the seaside have always been about wandering around rock pools and exploring fascinating beach detritus – wood, old ropes or polystyrene – that the sea had eroded and corroded and made beautiful. That gave us the confidence to make a building that we believe genuinely relates to the sea.

EAST BEACH CAFÉ

The Guardian *started a global newspaper design revolution in 1988 with David Hillman's iconic work. Mark Porter had the task of doing it all again for the 21st century. He asked Paul Barnes to design a new typeface.*

Mark Porter: As the Internet grows and free media becomes more available, the printed newspaper market is going to shrink. Our readers' lives are changing and the younger generation gets much of its information on-line. Since the millennium the "quality" newspapers have started making big changes.

The Independent went first in summer 2003 and The Times followed shortly after, pouring their newspapers into a tabloid format that was easier to handle, especially for commuters. To paraphrase Simon Kelner, they made different-sized tubes for the same toothpaste...The temptation in tabloid is to adopt a downmarket approach to the journalism, like loud headlines, mixing reporting with opinion and single-story front pages. The Guardian editor, Alan Rusbridger, wanted the new design to reflect the standards and values of broadsheet journalism. For us it was time to rethink the paper.

We went for a Berliner format, slightly larger than a tabloid. We've always been known as a writer's paper so we decided on five columns to make the text as readable as possible. We consciously tried to change the paper's pace by increasing the numbers of shorter and longer stories, moving away from the former, regular story length of around 450 words to introduce a more rhythmic approach. It was an 18-month development process involving everyone we could. The journalists, traditionally suspicious of designers, saw that we weren't trying to foist an aesthetic template on them, we were just trying to make the paper easier to read.

In our early enthusiasm we allowed ourselves to imagine that we'd turn around the declining newspaper market, but nothing is capable of doing that! We did, however, increase our market share. The Guardian was the first UK national to be colour throughout and the first to make amazing news images the regular centre spread picture – something that's now copied all over the world.

We did it to be a successful printed product, but, serendipitously, it's given us a new, vigorous identity and a strong visual voice with which to build our website and digital design. For me the most gratifying moment came when my father called me on the morning that the new design came out. At 77, he's a lifelong Guardian reader. He told me it was fantastic and that he had read it from the first page to the last; something he hadn't done for many years.

Paul Barnes: Type design is obsessive, it's all about perfection and details. I've always been interested in letters; my grandfather worked in newspapers, my mother was a calligrapher. As a teenager I was fascinated by lettering on album covers. I studied typography at university and would have probably followed the typical book design career path. But I met Roger Black at a conference and he offered me a job redesigning magazines. It was through him that I developed an interest in publication designing and the role of typography.

David Hillman's design had been a very influential piece of work. But as time went on it began to date; it was limited by the available Helvetica. When Mark first asked me to consult I suggested that we revise Helvetica, so I began working with type designer Christian Schwartz to make a version nearer to The Guardian's current needs. Christian and I then looked at a new serif typeface (which became Publico) but in the end we had cold feet. We decided to start from scratch.

We went off for the weekend determined to develop a new sans serif. I was reminded of something Matthew Carter had once showed me; a sans serif derived from a slab serif with the slabs removed. Suddenly I saw a way of creating a typeface that was The Guardian's own. I saw Mark on the Monday; the first thing he said was that the slab looked more interesting than the sans. We felt that with a slab we could get some of the weight of a sans, but also some of the delicacy of a serif.

So now came the really hard work for Christian and me. Designing a typeface is a bit like sculpture – you chip away to ensure that all letters can work together in whatever order they're put on the page. You can never get it perfect, but in your effort to, you spend immense amounts of time positioning the letters against each other, swapping them,

refining them, repositioning them, moving on to the next group... The result, after many many months of work, was The Guardian typeface; Guardian Egyptian, Guardian Sans, Guardian Text Egyptian, Guardian Text Sans and Guardian Agate. The Egyptian is used for headlines and display, Text for the copy, and Agate we used for financial figures and sports results. The journalists loved it because they could get more words on a page.

The fear before the redesign was that we were going to get it wrong. But the reaction was perfect. At first, no one batted an eyelid! Typography is pretty silent, so if it's good, people don't notice. They could feel, "oh, this is still our Guardian". It's not better than Hillman's work, it's just different. His came from the '80s; this design is made in this age. Typefaces reflect times and forge fashions.

ABCDEF
GHIJKLMN
OPQRSTU
VWXYZ
1234567890
abcdefghij
klmnopqrst
uvwxyz

the**guardian** Saturday | 03.12.05 | guardian.co.uk/sport   Christian O'Connell's iconic gripes page 16 »

sport

the**guardian** Saturday 03.12.05 | guardian.co.uk   How big a tart are you? » Page 10

money

Win a top-of-the-range travel system » Pa...

Turner's pension prize
The solution to the pensions crisis is working until 68 and a new national savings scheme, says Lord Turner. But can the low-paid really afford to shell out £60 a month? » Page 4

the**guardian** Saturday 05.11.05 | guardian.co.uk   A life in writing – Michel Houellebecq » Page 11

review

...arnes

the**guardian** Saturday 26.11.05 | guardian.co.uk/work   Labour's workplace hits and misses » Page 5   ...w Motion on Anthony Powell » Page 14

work

the**guardian** Saturday 12.11.05 | guardian.co.uk   All this and opera too in Sydney » Page 4   ...essential section for...   When grandparents are left holding the baby » Page 4

travel   family

Vic Falls, Livingstone-style » Page 7

Fes of the heart
by William Dalrymple

...the family » Page 8

the guide
the**guardian**

Streets ahead
The ghetto kids who danced their way to fam...

❋ **Been there?** Think you...
by sending us your tips f...

guardian
WEEKEND
15.10.05

PLUS
BIROTLU
JET9 WALL
MAD DOGS

Free DVD

WIDESCREEN
BAGDAD CAFE
the**guardian**

Christmas books
Chosen by Beryl Bainbridge, Julian Barnes, David Hare, Zadie Smith and others
Review

the guardian
1946-2005
£1.30
Saturday 26.11.05
Published in London and Manchester
guardian.co.uk

Column five
Life's game, as played by George Best

Richard Williams

Best in 1966, the year in which he scored two goals in Manchester United's 5-1 European Cup quarter-final victory over Benfica Photograph: Ray Green/Popperfoto

Continued on page 2 »

National	National	International	Financial	Sport
PC's murder: police name wanted men		**Blair steps into Uganda poll row**	**Sales growth slows at Tesco**	**Ballack says no to Old Trafford**

...ant? Get a dog!

...ant was adamant she did not want
...ry, the Portuguese water dog?

Photography: Amit Lennon

...online, email or write to us
...y, 119 Farringdon Road, London EC1R 3ER

The Roundhouse in Camden, London, is a world-famous performance venue, which, in its heyday, hosted the likes of Pink Floyd, the Stones, Hendrix, Bowie and Zeppelin. After a long period of decline, a visionary new owner commissioned McAslan and Partners to renew and refresh this unique building.

John McAslan:
The toy magnate Torquil Norman bought the Roundhouse in the late '90s and used his resources to embark upon a fund-raising exercise aimed at turning the former railway turntable shed into a performance centre.

His vision was to create a dynamic environment to get young people in off the streets to record and perform music, develop their creative skills and put them to good use. So our mission was to design a creative engine that could serve the local community and actually help turn lives around. The plan grew as the business case developed alongside new funding sources. In the end Torquil raised some £20 million from a standing start.

Our work focused on returning the central rotunda to its former glory as a performance space. At one point Torquil wanted to put in another deck but we discussed it with him and in the end he agreed it would have destroyed the dramatic view upwards.

Standing in the middle of the Roundhouse is spectacular; it's a fantastic space to be in. And it's great to see it back in use.

We also had to develop the basement, or undercroft, into studios for film and music. To do all this we decided we needed a separate building for additional features, like bars and restaurants, which we built in a quarter arc around the northwest side of the building, connected by a sweeping walkway; we called it the Radial Wing.

The existing building and the radial wing are separated by the curving processional stairway that creates a sweeping circulatory route. It provides a clear delineation between new and old, the new having a big public face on Chalk Farm Road, and the old retaining the solidity of the engine shed.

Apart from the central rotunda, I think the sweeping stairway is the most successful part of the design. It's a dramatic experience walking up through the old and into the new, all bathed in that fantastic light coming through the atrium, revealing the rawness of the original design.

THE ROUNDHOUSE

SUBVERSION

ISLE OF HARRIS, SCOTLAND

Simon Waterfall and Matthew "Tig" Grey believe that men's clothing has been far too boring for far too long. They believe good suits tell stories, and they subvert them with witty touches like razors, pheasants and even the Queen. They call their business Social Suicide, but they've been selling all around the world.

Simon Waterfall: Compared to women's, men's fashion is soooo dull. Men buy suits like they buy their aftershave – they choose the one they least hate. Social Suicide is a reaction to that. Wearing our suits might be risky, but haven't women already proved that risky clothes are the most fun?

In 2004 I was asked to introduce Her Majesty to the top 500 designers in the UK. If you're meeting the Queen, you've got to make an effort, so we designed a special suit for the occasion. I said: "Ma'am, I've been asked to show you my suit, but to do so I'm going to have to do something my father said I should never do." I then walked away and turned my back on her.

There was a moment of silence and then she laughed: "Marvellous! How long did it take?"

"Seven episodes of *Neighbours*," I told her. "And we've been really generous," I added, "we've based it on a stamp from 1970; you look really young!"

"Very Pearly King," she said, and she was right: the image is made up of 620 different-sized pearl buttons.

We take pride in making our suits to really high standards. We use tailors in India who take a full day to make each suit. We cut the patterns on Savile Row using Joe Morgan, who was Tommy Nutter's pattern cutter. Each suit is individually numbered.

In a recent autumn collection we made the Teddy – a jacket inspired by the Teddy boys. They used to sew razorblades under their lapels, so if you grabbed them to "nut" them, you regretted it... We've stitched solid silver razorblades into ours; blunt, admittedly, though still not airline-friendly.

Then there's the Shark Jacket, with slitted gills down the sides that flare open when you lift your arms in anger; it took months to get the gills to lie flat.

Or the John Holmes Suit complete with a tape measure to suggest 14 inches of fun... Or the Poacher's Jacket with a pheasant embroidered on the inside...

As you can imagine, Tig and I have had a great time thinking these up... and we love the reactions, suggestions and stories we get on the website.

THE PEARLY QUEEN SUIT

The National Gallery found itself fighting a prejudice that was stopping some people from coming through their doors. They turned to The Partners for help.

Jim Prior: The gallery felt it had lack of relevance amongst Londoners who might have recognised Tate Modern as attractive but didn't think they could engage with Old Masters. It wasn't that these people were coming to the gallery and leaving disappointed; they just weren't coming. So our brief was to coax them over the perceptional threshold.

The idea for the Grand Tour came out of a series of brainstorms. It was a bit "mountain and Mohammed" – if the people won't come to the art, bring the art to the people. We proposed it as one of six strategies; I think they chose it for its drama and appropriateness.

The serendipity of it was that Hewlett Packard, who were already involved with the gallery, had created a library of super-high-resolution digital images of the entire collection. They also recently developed a graffiti-proof printing material which could withstand all weather conditions.

Greg Quinton: We knew that just by putting the paintings on the streets they'd automatically be startling and arresting. We had to be really careful to avoid undermining the integrity of the painting. That wasn't easy; plenty of Old Masters have suffered from being featured in poster campaigns. So we mitigated that by putting them in appropriate picture frames.

Choosing the 44 sites (and getting the necessary permissions) was quite a job. We wanted to make sure each painting would work with its context without creating inappropriate gags. We put tranquil paintings in busy environments – *Whistlejacket* by Stubbs appeared on a huge brick wall in Endell Street; the red brick almost "played" with the reds and browns of the horse. And Caravaggio was next to a Soho sex shop; a subtle reference to the artist's own racy lifestyle. The client was delighted. Some 28,000 leaflets were picked up from the gallery by people who had seen the paintings over 12 weeks, and it's currently touring the UK.

Controlled
ZONE

Mon - Sat
8.30 am - 6.30 pm

JEEVES AND WOOSTER LIGHT

Jake Phipps sees himself as a problem-solver, and the more bizarre the problem, the more he likes it. Inspired by a competition, he combined Magritte with PG Wodehouse to say something quintessentially British.

Jake Phipps: I'm a member of Hidden Art, a collective for new designers based in London's East End. As part of a launch event, Hidden Art asked us to come up with designs for a range of products that they would later market. The brief was pretty open: the products should reflect Britishness with a contemporary feel.

As a trained cabinetmaker I had never really designed anything other than furniture, but I had this yearning to design a light. And this yearning married with another of my recent obsessions: hats. I was fascinated by the way hats can so easily demonstrate the wearer's cultural identity. The bowler hat is a classic – its nuances come out in the character of Jeeves, who exudes a flair for intelligent but hard-working style in a quintessentially British manner. Wooster sums up the "high-class fun" meanings in the top hat.

I think my idea owes something to Magritte's *Son of Man*, the one with the man in a bowler with an apple hovering in front of his face. I made the hats into absurd lights. There's something eccentric about a hat hanging from the ceiling as if its owner has dissolved beneath it, or as if it has just been thrown into the air.

They are made from real hats with a hole drilled in the top for the light fitting. The bowler's lining is made of bronze and brass, the top hat features a more imperious polished silver. They're in a Philippe Starck hotel in Paris and Tommy Hilfiger has them in a window display in Amsterdam.

I loved the whole process: taking a found object, turning it on its head and putting it into a different environment while keeping the original aesthetic. It's a nice thing to do!

It isn't often that designers have a vicar for a client. When Marksteen Adamson was asked by the vicar of St Kea to rebrand his church near Truro in Cornwall, he decided to capture people's attention by getting them to smile.

Marksteen Adamson: Christian marketing can be embarrassing; especially when it tries to be trendy or shocking. I knew we had to do a lot better than: "Sex! Now that I have your attention let me tell you about Jesus…"

There are few brands more loaded than Christianity; it carries the sort of luggage that can make Christians reluctant to advertise their beliefs. But the vicar of St Kea, Adrian Hallett, took the opposite view. "Christianity can help and support people in lots of different ways," he told me, "but the public just doesn't see it. This church needs to be heard in this community, because it's relevant. We have a lot to offer that is being ignored."

That was the brief: St Kea had to be more "heard" and appear more relevant. I felt it was really important that the campaign had a contemporary feel and I wanted to use humour by reclaiming some blasphemy and putting it back into "the kingdom of God".

So Scott McGuffie and I started thinking about products that could both raise money and deliver an engaging message; domestic items that would be easily seen and would attract comment. We came up with "Pennies from Heaven" on a piggybank, "Heavens Above" on an umbrella, "More Tea Vicar?" on a mug. We've even designed a bread tin that will mould the phrase "Daily Bread" into the bread itself, and a T-shirt with the word "T-shirt" as the breast logo, but with the T formed as a crucifix.

It's all had quite an impact. People would come into the church off the street because they'd seen the products and decided that St Kea's must be friendly. Blogs in America picked up on it and we got calls from around the world asking for the products. And lo, Richard and Judy saw that it was good, and it came to pass that ITV descended among us… And then it all went a bit mad. St Kea's was inundated with orders and a poor old lady from the church found herself struggling to send out umbrellas and tissue boxes to destinations around the world!

HOLY SMOKE
…Non drip candles

'Holy Smoke' is the registered trademark of God's Kingdom ltd

ST KEA IDENTITY

SiKea
THE BUSINESS OF LIFE

GOD BLESS YOU +
...Just reach out

Cadbury was faced with a gradual year-on-year decline for its flagship brand, Cadbury's Dairy Milk. They went to Fallon Advertising to turn it round. Partner Chris Willingham oversaw the account.

Chris Willingham: Cadbury had a new marketing director, Phil Rumbol, who had previously been in charge of the "reassuringly expensive" Stella Artois series, set in turn-of-the-century France, and he was open to radical change.

Cadbury had been using traditional persuasion techniques to try and win people over to Dairy Milk: the product and the promise were quite overt and, it might be argued, a little mechanical in the way fast-moving consumer goods advertising has a habit of being. He encouraged us to change the whole approach. He was concerned not only about the decline in Dairy Milk sales, but the fact that Britain seemed to be losing its love for what was a bit of an institution – it was time to blow off some of the dust.

We only had a week to come up with a concept, so we didn't have time to be frightened by what was a very open brief. We had the usual brainstorming sessions, which generated three ideas, two of which were all about a world of chocolate like you'd never seen before. The third didn't involve the product until the end, when up pops the chocolate with the legend "A glass and a half full of joy."

The idea for the third approach came from the question "What do people like about chocolate?" and the answer, "that it brings you a little piece of happiness during the day". In this sense, Cadbury are manufacturing good times; it was an interesting step. So we made it our mission to produce ads that made people feel as good as when they eat the chocolate. And so the "Glass and a Half Full Productions" concept was born – as well as delivering an emotional

promise it also allowed us to deliver a rational product message, drawing attention to the fact that Cadbury used a glass and a half of real milk versus competitors who use powdered milk.

We knew that we had to find something original and unexpected; well, that's what ads should always do. It had to deliver this joy in a way that wasn't too earnest, nor too mechanical or manufactured. So we started brainstorming things that would make us happy. A creative, Juan Cabral, said: "Look, I've always wanted to be able to play the drum roll in the beginning of Phil Collins's *In the Air Tonight*. It would be a great moment if I could play that!" It was the beginning of a perfect idea. The intro to that track has a real build to it with lyrics to reflect the anticipation – "I've been waiting for this moment for all my life, oh Lord" – and gives you enough time to study the character and engage with the gorilla, to catch the gold tooth you can see when he aggressively curls his lip, to see him stretch his neck, to see him close his eyes, taking in the music… By the time he hits the drums, you are there on the drum seat with him. We knew that we needed that level of detail – it was absolutely critical in order to really take hold.

Why a gorilla? There's no real logic; it just works and it's visually fascinating. And it wasn't as if it was a tiger or a giraffe; it was believable – so much so, in fact, that the YouTube commentary that followed was full of people asking how we'd trained the gorilla to do it! It was a man in a suit, of course; it took us two months to find the best gorilla suit in the world – we got it from Hollywood.

When the clients saw the Gorilla ad, they couldn't stop smiling. It was launched in 2007 during the final of Big Brother, and the YouTube version scored a million hits in the first week. The sales uplift was some 9 per cent, and since then the trend has been upwards. The ads have been spoofed by Alan Carr and Lily Allen amongst many others; spoofs are often a really good sign…

The Angel of the North has become a much-loved iconic sculpture – so it was inevitable that someone would produce a subversive souvenir.

Kit Grover: Well of course this version of the Angel of the North is a deeply important conceptual piece… but amazingly people just think it's a bit of light-hearted memento fun.

When you take a famous image and you reduce it or change it for commercial purpose, it can look like you've squeezed the life and soul out of it. Little Eiffel Towers, models of the Houses of Parliament, St Paul's in a snowstorm, etc. So we try to add a little humour.

Why a wooden toy of the Angel of the North? It's basically saying that the sculpture has passed into the culture, has become ingrained in the UK national consciousness. It's just a little fun commemorative that isn't too worthy. You press the button on the bottom and it falls over. Ha ha! And then you let the button go, and hey, it stands up. We even do a balsa aeroplane, complete with rubber band, in the shape of the Angel of the North. It flies pretty well, given that the wings are so long…

I'm not sitting around and trying to be subversive, but it is always interesting to see what happens to things when they are moved out of their protected environments and respectable settings. In the art world, shops are not really considered respectable, even though artists depend on them (but artists do have lots of issues…). We just try to walk a funny line between commerce and art. It's often quite instinctive.

For example, we do all the merchandise for the Royal Shakespeare Company. *Flipping Shakespeare!* is a series of flip-books based on the plays. And we make wooden Shakespeare toys like Caesar with a knife in his back and Hamlet carrying a skull and a shovel. We've also made some silly things for the Royal Collection, who wanted to modernise their catalogue. So we made some gear for corgis – a camp black-and-pink dog bowl, a sort of bondage collar and lead… and, for the dog's owner, a foam crown.

ANGEL OF THE NORTH TOY

I had my first design studio in Covent Garden right opposite the underground station, so I loved Stephen Jones's Tube Hat.

Stephen Jones: The basic thing about design and the creative process is that it's almost always autobiographical; any designer who says it isn't, is a fibber! You can't do good design in the third person; it has to have personal resonance and personal connection – that's where the passion comes from.

I've been working around Covent Garden for my whole working life; it's always been in my soul. My first studio was in Langley Street and here I am, just up the road in Great Queen Street, some 29 years later. It's a great place, full of all life. Like 42nd Street, Covent Garden is "where the underworld meets the elite"; the Opera House and the old Flower Market used to be cheek by jowl. And it's the home of great music clubs like the Roxy and the Vortex. So among the flower hats and top hats, I thought about representing how you get to and from Covent Garden. Hence the Taxi Hat and the Tube Hat.

Designed by Edward Johnston in 1917, the famous Underground logo is circular, so a miniature beret was right. The strap around the back of the head is based on the wonderful 1931 map designed by Harry Beck. There's something slightly naïve about those colours, they're somehow childish and exhilarating. We've reversed all the colours for legal reasons...

Hat design is always a leap of faith; you can never be sure if it will work out well. People say that inspired design is 90 per cent perspiration and 10 per cent inspiration. But they always forget the element of luck – that element of serendipity that brings all the thoughts and craft together and makes it work. The thing about hats is that, ultimately, they are just eye-candy; they've got to look like a great hat first.

This was a balancing act between the height and the width and the different panels of felt. Like Schiaparelli's Shoe Hat, the balance has to be right, or it just looks daft.

The Tube Hat's proved very popular; I've sold it to clients from New York to Hong Kong. Somehow it's optimistic and funny in a way that the London Underground definitely isn't!

THE TUBE HAT

Each year Michael Wolff creates a calendar of cartoons for his client 3i. It's a gift their customers look forward to receiving. But the cartoons are not just about making you laugh – the aim is to touch you deeper than that...

Michael Wolff: Paradoxically, perhaps, the inspiration behind the 3i Calendar is the world of finance. People in the money business tend to take life extremely seriously and usually consider money no laughing matter. But money is always dealt with in the context of relationships, and relationships are a laughing matter, among, of course, the many other things that they are.

Through their investment business 3i deal with the intimate aspects of people's personal lives, aspirations and ambitions, so, despite the coldness of money, there is already the potential for a closer relationship. Humour is a tremendous catalyst for open and honest relationships: if you laugh with a client you can be more open and relaxed and you can find, more easily, common strands and experiences. Business is based on trust, intuition and analysis and other left-brain stuff. So it's a good balance to introduce into the relationship right-brain activities that are happening in the here and now, like humour. Put simply, if you laugh with your client, you'll both feel more open and relaxed.

Those thoughts inspired me to find a way to put 3i into the minds of those who they wanted to think well of them. When I started the calendar I used cartoons from *Punch*, which were instantly funny. But I changed tack after I saw some cartoons in the *New Yorker*. Here was a different sense of humour, one that touches more intimately. I remember the first one that struck me was by Charles Barsotti. It featured a little man with two thought bubbles. The first read: "What's next?" and the second: "Don't tell me!" To me, the cartoon captures those fundamental fears we all have, and it just made me chuckle. There's another, I think by Peter Mueller, which features a cat waiting outside a mouse hole. In exasperation the cat says: "Alright then, live in darkness!" – a perfect summing up of that unreasonable feeling we can all have when things don't go according to our plans, all because other people have their own (quite understandable) agendas.

I've done the 3i Calendar for 21 years – that's over a thousand cartoons. Each one, I think, touches someone, somewhere, "surgically" – deep inside – helping them to laugh at their own, and other people's, attitudes. *New Yorker* cartoons are deeper than just funny. And, for 3i, it's a way of saying: "Look, we understand how people really are." Which is not what you'd expect, perhaps, from people whose core business is investing money.

Mon	Tue	Wed	Thu	Fri	Sat	Sun
20	21	22	23	24	25	26

February

NB: Studio were asked to create a piece of work for the 2006 London Design Festival that would celebrate London. They chose to take the A–Z street atlas, one of London's icons, and give it a typographical twist.

Nick Finney: We were approached by the International Society for Typographic Designers to create a piece of work based on the theme "My London, My City". It was pretty much an open brief. Given it was coming from the ISTD we figured it might be best if we did something about typography. So we ummed and we ahhhed and drew various sketches and the thing that came out of our scribbles was: What about the A–Z street map of London? Everyone's got one and it's a bit of an icon; it's been around since 1936. Why don't we just strip everything out, the borders, the colour, and just leave the typography?

Straight away it gave us a black and white map rather than a full colour assault on the eyes, and it removed the division that is the river, appearing to bring the two halves of the city much closer together. And there were bare spaces here and there, often parks, or possibly contaminated land... The idea was to squeeze and "kern" the letters into the form of streets and roads. So we called it *London's Kerning*, a pun on the old round "London's Burning" and, of course, the Clash song.

It was all happenstance uncovered by working through a problem in the way we do best. And it was a labour of love! We assumed we'd just be able to go to the A–Z website and download the artwork, or we'd be able to buy the A–Z CD, open it up in Adobe Illustrator and switch off various layers. But unfortunately the artwork was a photograph... So myself, Alan Dye, Ben Stott and team, landed up taking the A–Z apart and laying it out in squares; it's not often you have a reason to do that. We scanned them in to the computer and wiped away the extraneous detail, leaving just the type. So that was a few late nights... There are, we must admit, a few typos here and there, where someone must have inadvertently wiped a letter off a street name.

We decided to print it as a poster and it became this thing that people wanted to put on their walls and champion on their blogs. We did one that was 60 x 40 inches – the biggest size we could realistically get printed by traditional means... At the time we were asked by *Wallpaper* to submit a twist on a popular game for their December edition. We came back with some rude card games, but they preferred to see a giant jigsaw puzzle of the map. The result was a fiendishly difficult interpretation of our *London's Kerning* poster, made from wood.

LONDON'S KERNING

Artist and designer Helen David is the founder of the English Eccentrics label, which she set up with her husband, Colin. Helen's created a delightfully evocative series of candles, designed to set a particular mood.

Helen David:
The theme for these candles is based on the sensations you might have in a fairytale. Enchanted Forest, for example, evokes the smells of a fairytale woodcutter's cottage; it's rich and smoky with an incense-like scent of cedar wood and birch. Eccentricity, which shows a stylised London cityscape on the packaging, evokes the feel of riding through Hyde Park on a spring morning. The scent is an English twist on cologne, with bergamot, petitgrain and herbs touched with a hint of saddle leather. Another is Secret Garden: it gives off the aroma of gardenia, tuberose and jasmine, evoking the heady scent of a 1920s conservatory.

For Tea with the Queen, I tried to imagine what it would be like to have tea at Buckingham Palace. I thought that the Queen might choose to have Devon violets on her table, they're classic English flowers and unpretentious (as I believe she is). This is mixed with the scent of Darjeeling tea to reflect the closeness of India to the history of the Crown. The graphics feature the lion and the unicorn, and, of course, teapots and tea cups. It's also inspired by the AA Milne poem that begins, "They're changing guard at Buckingham Palace – Christopher Robin went down with Alice…" Going to the palace to meet the Queen; there's something sweet about it. It's a very popular candle!

I see scents as somehow having colours, and the packaging and candle colours reflect how I think they would look if the scents were colours. The whole series is made in Cornwall by a specialist candle manufacturer.

TEA WITH THE QUEEN CANDLES

scented candle

TEA WITH THE QUEEN
English Eccentrics™

HUMANISM

ST MICHAEL'S MOUNT, CORNWALL, ENGLAND

The charity Leonard Cheshire took advantage of some highly creative thinking from Freud Communications and Aardman Animations to help people understand how difficult life can be for disabled people.

Steve Harding-Hill: I'd never been asked to do a classic Wallace and Gromit style job at Aardman; it just wasn't my kind of thing. So when my boss asked me to do this project, I said, apprehensively, "OK".

The idea came from Dave Waters and Simon Riley at Freud Communications, who proposed the Creature Discomforts concepts to their clients, the disability charity Leonard Cheshire. They'd put together a sample script and it really was quite "out there". After meeting them and seeing the script I was all fired up.

So off we went, armed with a digital sound recorder, to do interviews at Leonard Cheshire homes around the country. We asked the interviewees about the three As: what Access problems they had, what Attitudes people had to disability and what Actions they thought should be taken to improve things.

Then we had to choose which animals should represent the voices, and what scenarios to put them in. That meant trawling through some 40 hours of audio and whittling it down to about 20 possibles; that took about a fortnight. We needed to get a good mix of gender, age and type of disability.

We use audio rather than video for the recordings; we find it works much better if we have to imagine what the interviewees look like and it's fun to conjure up the face and the animal that suits the voice. The choices are instinctive, really. The stick insect was easy, because it was about a man walking with a stick!

One interview was about a blind man who, as a child, had such poor peripheral vision his classmates could sneak up from the side and whack him because he couldn't see them coming. His story made me think of a chameleon (they have swivel eyes and can see in all sorts of directions). So, a chameleon with really bad peripheral vision just seemed like a good idea. Later we gave him a ladybird as a guide dog. That's the fun of it, those little extra details. The chameleon, being a bit blind, doesn't look at the camera, but the ladybird does, engaging the audience. A favourite moment is when the chameleon catches the fly that walks on the camera lens and so into his field of vision. The plasticine tongue we used was 2 metres long! It was great getting the sound of the "ting!" of the tongue hitting the glass and the squelch of the fly…

Leonard Cheshire were great clients; really responsive to the new ideas we built in as we went along. Of course, on a stop-motion shoot like this, time is always a factor; you always wish you had more. But sometimes time pressure does force you to make better creative decisions…

CREATURE DISCOMFORTS

Do you hate electric hand dryers in washrooms? If so, James Dyson has come up with a design that will completely change your mind.

James Dyson: I had a dread of going into a washroom and finding an electric hand dryer. You wash your hands, walk over to this thing, put your hands under it, rub them for a bit in a stream of warm smelly air, get bored, wipe your hands on your trousers and walk out. You'd feel dirtier than before you went in. Airblade came out of the sheer frustration and annoyance of those dreadful things...

The basic technology for the Airblade has been around for a while; you see it in the car wash when the water is blown off your car. We were developing "air knife" technology for another project, when someone had a wet hand and decided to wipe the air knife across it. The thin blast of air acted like a windscreen wiper.

Serendipity played a big part, because at the time we started thinking about applying the air knife to washrooms, we were also developing a new motor for our vacuum cleaners that does over 100,000rpm. We thought that if we used the new motor to run an air-compression fan we could generate massive pressure and force higher volumes of air through a thin slot. We made a slot just 0.3mm wide, and, with the new motor, we were able to force the air through at some 400 miles an hour.

The Airblade takes around 10 seconds to dry small hands – bigger hands dry quicker because they are closer to the air blades. You just lower your hands slowly into the airstream and then gradually withdraw them. And, hey presto, they're dry. Before Airblade there was no real standard for how dry hands are. So we worked with the National Sanitation Foundation of the United States to create a standard.

We made several prototypes before deciding we needed to filter the air – the idea of blowing warm unclean lavatory air over our hands was not appealing! The filters take out 99.9 per cent of germs. We also worked hard to make it as vandal-proof as possible. We even had to make it vomit-proof! And because we don't need to heat up the air, we use far less power. It means fewer contaminated paper towels going into landfill, and a smaller carbon footprint all round. People who use them commercially tell us Airblade is saving them significant amounts of money.

It's a bit of a departure for us, and we do have to learn to operate in this new market, but it's been doing very well. Clearly this isn't anything like as high volume as the domestic market, though we are considering a home version; the kitchen is the obvious place because the towel you use there is probably a fairly foul thing once it's got a few bits of old food on it. And yes, we are thinking of employing similar technology in a shower; for some reason that idea's been suggested to me by every American I've met! No more soggy towels...

DYSON AIRBLADE HAND DRYER

Widely considered to be the new barometer of fashion, Natalie Massenet's on-line shopping magazine, NET-A-PORTER.COM, has revolutionised the way people around the world buy designer clothes. It is also one of the fastest-growing businesses in the UK.

Natalie Massenet: I had been a fashion editor for many years and had dreamt of being the editor of my own fashion magazine. Back then we photographed everything new and exciting but when it came time to tell our readers how they could buy what they were looking at, we often found that the stores hadn't bought the pieces. They'd say they were too avant-garde or weren't the sort of thing that had sold in the past. I realised there was a disconnect between fashion media creating excitement and retail stockists.

This thought sat at the back of my head until the day, in 1999, that I fell in love with the computer. I spent all day browsing the web; it was a mind explosion! You could type something in and get swept away on a wave of connected links. The shopping potential seemed enormous. It was the time of the dot.com bubble and everyone was talking about Amazon. I just assumed it already existed for fashion. But, to my amazement, the big fashion brands weren't delivering globally on-line.

As a journalist I was trained to think about what's next. To me this was a giant, blinking, neon sign shouting Opportunity! But when I talked to

friends in the fashion business they stared at me blankly – it simply wasn't on their radar. I was convinced that it needed to happen now; creative thinking is important, but delivering the ideas is even more important. So I said to a fashion brand, over lunch: "Give me your product and I'll put it on the Internet and make it look like a fashion magazine." They said OK.

My husband, an investment banker, explained how you could raise money on a good business idea before you'd built the company, that you could build a business based on future valuations. Originally I wanted a business I could run from my kitchen table. My first brand idea was *What's New PussyCat?*, an on-line magazine from which you could order direct. I went to see a lawyer to register the brand and he said: "I can't trademark this! Come up with something else that won't attract the wrong kind of traffic..." I spent three days thinking about it but there was a real "land grab" going on for good Internet names and there was very little left. Out of desperation I went to a fashion dictionary and worked through to prêt-à-porter, ready-to-wear. I thought "net-a-porter", for shopping on the net. No one else had thought to register it, so I worried that it was a bad idea. It took a week of ignoring it before the lightbulb suddenly flashed.

Then everything really crystallised. If it was going to feature collections from Milan, Paris, New York and London, then NET-A-PORTER.COM had to be a big brand itself: it had to be slick, global and luxurious. That set the tone and pace for

everything to come: the packaging became black and timeless and the website became more chic. Suddenly the business plan was all about global, long-term growth. As we got to work I was constantly concerned that everyone in the fashion business was working on the same idea and that we'd be swept away by rivals at launch.

Keeping ahead of the game is absolutely key. We have a fantastic in-house design team and they generate a great creative feeling; for us, the lowest depth of misery is to be in the same place as everyone else. So, to keep fresh, we'll go visually to a place that may feel awkward at first but at least it's new. A few months later it becomes a standard and everyone's copying us again.

I'm very bullish on new technology. We're ten years in but it's still Day One of the Internet revolution. And, because the Internet is global, it's not so subject to local fluctuations: on-line businesses have a much better chance of staying stable and acquiring new customers.

My nine-year-old daughter loves fashion, but she doesn't really know what it means to go shopping in a store on a Saturday. To her, shopping means scrolling down, pointing at what she likes, getting a close-up of the fabric, and having it delivered the next day. When she's old enough to shop on her own it's likely to be from her mobile phone and she'll be able to show all her friends what's she's bought. As more consumers migrate on-line, there are going to be many more blinking neon signs that shout Opportunity!

NET-A-PORTER.COM

This project was part of joinedupdesignforschools, in which pupils from across the UK worked closely with designers to improve their schools. Twelve- to fourteen-year-old pupils in Falmouth wanted a new Design and Technology studio.

Alex Mowat:
This new £500,000 Design and Technology studio is a timber structure with a sawtooth roof that brings an even north light into the space. Urban Salon got the project after the Sorrell Foundation put us in touch with Falmouth School in Cornwall. The pupils could have chosen to improve their uniform, redesign their toilets or improve their school logo, but they felt that their DT building was most in need of a designer. It's right at the front of the school and was no longer fit for purpose, having been built when DT was all about sawing and welding. They didn't want their computers and drawing-boards next to dusty, greasy pillar drills; they wanted a modern, eco-friendly studio space that would also be a local landmark.

We brought the young client team to London to see a working design studio complete with clean computers, big plotters and creative meeting rooms. And so began the conversation, a relationship that, in the end, lasted some years. We spent two days in London with the original team, taking them on a journey through design from office furniture showrooms right up the scale to city planning. Catching the number 12 bus down to Peckham to stand outside the new library in the rain to discuss what works is definitely a bonding experience. We should do more of it with our other clients...

They didn't define a budget in their first brief. So we gave them four options at different scales and they rejected the smaller ones as not fulfilling the "landmark" criterion. They were very good at deciding what materials would survive the school environment, and they were strong on making decisions about where best to spend the money and where to save it. We chose the black and yellow colour scheme with the client team to represent the Cornish crest. We also refurbished the five existing workshops, solving their overheating problems. And we've just heard that they've received planning permission for a wind turbine. It's been a great relationship.

It's the airiness of the space that I love. You get these slot views out to the trees and landscape, and yet, even with 1,500 students shouting and running outside at the end of the school day, you can still work quietly in a calm, light environment. We've managed to connect to the space outside without putting the pupils on show. It's a good balance.

FALMOUTH SCHOOL

Scientists at Blatchford have developed the Echelon: a new generation of prosthetic foot that makes it easier for amputees to walk up and down slopes and hills – and even make a parachute jump.

David Moser:
There is a strong medical need for a prosthetic foot that can adapt to different angles. When a natural foot pushes against a slope, it makes automatic adjustments in response to the angle – 26 bones and over 30 joints combine effortlessly to correct your alignment. But with a prosthetic foot you can't adjust that alignment and the ground seems to push back awkwardly and unnaturally, making it impossible for an amputee to stand or walk on a slope in a natural way. This can lead to health problems.

Most modern prosthetic feet are made of very efficient spring materials, but they really only work for one alignment and one walking (or running) speed. The Echelon breaks the mould of current design philosophies and is much more capable of having a massive effect on quality of life.

The solution we've come up with combines hydraulics with sprung composites to form a viscose-elastic system which mimics some of the biomechanical and adaptive properties of the muscles and so allows improved comfort, balance and safety. By putting the hydraulics on top of the foot we were able, for the first time, to instantly optimise the alignment of the body with the ground in a way that happens automatically on every step. It was a great team effort.

Graham Harris:
The industry had experimented with hydraulic ankles before; the biggest problems were to do with the complexity and size of the previous solutions. We were looking for a small, lightweight, robust, durable solution based on composite leaf springs and simple hydraulics. One of the most challenging aspects of the design was the marrying of the foot spring elements to the hydraulic ankle movement. Simply adding a full range of ankle movement to the springs can lead to too much movement, so the goal was to harmonise the two systems.

The final design solution uses a small hydraulic piston with a pair of control valves so that the angular movement of the foot can be independently adjusted to make it suitable for a range of amputees and activities. The piston has a limited travel so that, during the gait cycle, loads are transferred correctly to the heel and toe springs. A full range of springs is available to suit individual amputees. We did a lot of experimentation around the biomechanics of a balanced system.

Fadi Abimosleh:
We first worked on adjustable heel alignment in an earlier product, the Brio. It consisted of a hydraulic cylinder that allowed you to adjust the alignment of leg relative to the foot at the foot/ground interface and employed a valve to lock this alignment. We took that device and modified the valve so it could adjust the stiffness (or flexion) in the ankle by controlling the flow of hydraulic oil. It's a setting that you manually adjust to suit the patient's activity or weight. We put units on trial but soon learnt it had to be simpler.

We also needed to design the valve to offer a range of resistance, and created several iterations before coming up with a version featuring a series of holes, the smallest of which is just 29,000th of an inch. The holes control the size of the hydraulic fluid apertures; when the valve is turned, one or two holes will close. Another challenge was stopping the oil seals from leaking.

Patients saw benefits right away: some said that it was life-changing, others that it was like getting their own leg back. One spoke of turning up at a concert and being able to stand for two hours on a sloped floor without discomfort – unheard of in a standard prosthetic. We've yet to find someone who wants to give it back! The insights gained from this project have opened the door for future improvements.

ECHELON PROSTHETIC FOOT

Tobie Kerridge has developed a way of marrying biotechnology with jewellery design. Now you can have a wedding ring made from the very essence of your partner.

Tobie Kerridge: Nikki Stott and I were MA students at the Royal College of Art, and our mutual interest was biotechnology. We were given a brief asking us to use emerging materials technology in new design in such a way that encouraged interest and debate in new science. I'd developed an interest in tissue engineering; I loved the idea of growing bits of body in a lab and then using the results as a novel material for product design. Nikki and I began talking about the possibility of making jewellery from parts of the human body. To some this might sound macabre but to others there is something deeply romantic about having your wedding ring made from the very essence of your partner, their cells and their DNA.

We teamed up with Ian Thompson, a materials engineer at King's College, and we transformed our student brief into a funding application to the Engineering and Physical Sciences Research Council. They saw our work as an interesting way of promoting their desire to engage the public with new science. So, there we were, two designers and a tissue engineer, looking for a way to extend this into a real project with real people. We talked to the *New Scientist*, and, as a result of a piece they wrote, we got inquiries from some 200 couples! This project really was driven by the energy of that response.

We were aware that scientists were developing a way of growing bone in the laboratory; their aim is to grow big pieces to put back into a traumatised body, but they haven't quite got there yet; the scale is relatively small. We found two couples who were about to have work on their wisdom teeth, and persuaded them to let the oral surgeon remove a small chunk of their jawbone. We took the chunks to the lab, where they were ground down like a peppercorn to release the osteoblast cells, which are responsible for bone formation. The cells went into a nutritional culture to encourage them to multiply. Also in the culture was Ian's "bioactive scaffold", a pre-shaped ring form made of hydroxyapatite, which encourages the osteoblast cells to migrate into it, where they reproduce and grow throughout its porous structure. The scaffold degrades over some eight weeks, leaving a ring entirely grown from a small piece of your partner's jawbone...

I'm now doing a similar project called Material Beliefs, as part of a PhD at Goldsmith's College. Currently there are lots of these speculative design collaborations in which designers work with engineers and scientists all over the UK. I think it's a great way to explore the possibilities and engage people in emergent science.

BIO JEWELLERY

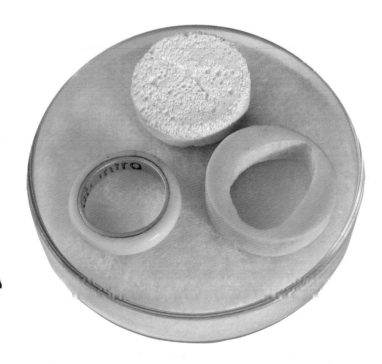

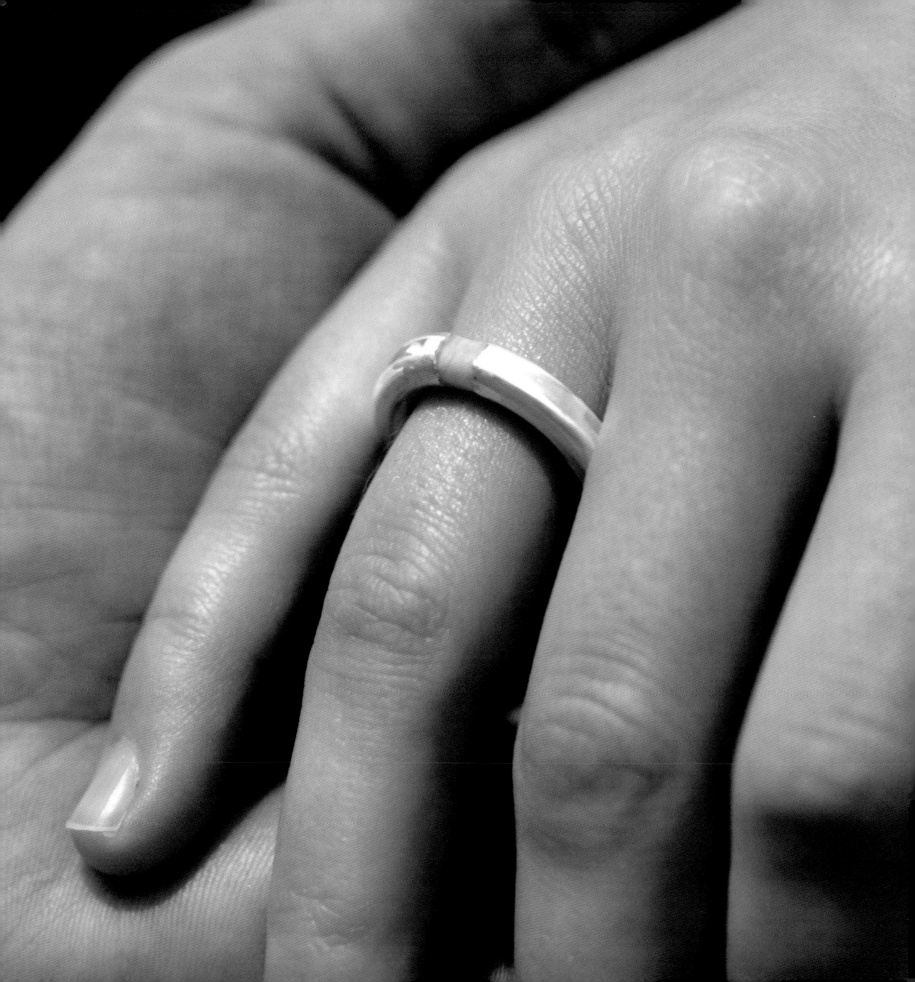

Tate Modern decided to mark its first rehang of all its major art with a performance piece, and approached Matt Clark of United Visual Artists, a new collective all about live performance and responsive installations.

Matt Clark: The brief was all about renewal and rebirth, and the whole concept of the piece is all about new life springing forth. So we decided to work with the acrobatic dance company Mimbre to create a "magical" experience... We installed a "Bumblebee2" stereo camera front of stage and projected live images from it on to a massive LED monolith on the end wall of the Turbine Hall. The camera filmed the dancers, and our software translated their moves into the more abstract, sculptural images on the screen. The stereo camera works like the human eye, so allowing us to create 3D images of the dancers and change viewing perspectives.

The piece begins with a display of something like spring blossom flying in the wind and falling from trees. These twisting clouds resolve into the moves that the performers are making on stage; it's as if their dancing souls have risen out of their bodies and are performing to an audience in a different dimension – a dreamlike sculptural expression of the dancers below.

One problem was designing the choreography within the limits of the camera's focal range, not easy given that the dancers have to get up speed for some of the acrobatics! And our rehearsal facilities weren't brilliant – we had to use our judgement on what would work within the massive Tate Turbine Hall.

It was pretty experimental, and the pressure was on to engage the audience and look spectacular. No one really knew what to expect. That's the attraction of doing such work – the creative freedom and the risk taking – in which everyone is involved. We found ourselves making features of the digital imperfections and mistakes...

Our thinking was all about grabbing things you take for granted and throwing them on their head; about looking at something familiar from a new perspective. I think that's where the appeal lay – in surprising people by this flowing, yet sculptural, instant interpretation of the Mimbre dancers.

ECHO

Chen Shi-Zheng is a New York-based director internationally renowned for his innovative and provocative staging of operas as diverse as Wagner's The Flying Dutchman *and Tang Xianzu's* The Peony Pavilion. *He also worked closely with Damon Albarn and Jamie Hewlett (from the virtual rock band Gorillaz) to create a stage production of* Monkey: Journey to the West, *which opened in Manchester in 2007. Jamie's drawings were inspired by his travels through China and the people he met and worked with on this grand projet.*

Jamie Hewlett:
Chen Shi-Zheng had always wanted to do a modern opera version of *Journey to the West*.
He and the Théâtre du Châtelet in Paris approached Alex Poots of the Manchester International Festival for funding. Alex had worked with Damon and me before and suggested that we collaborate. We ended up going to China with Shi-Zheng and Alex, where Shi-Zheng explained the story to us and why it was so important across Asia. It took two trips to China and lots of drawings before I began to get to a point where I was happy.

The first four months were complete confusion; it was quite scary doing this. But that's where the excitement is for me, the challenge. I guess our creative processes were different... I just drew lots of pictures for ages. Feedback from Shi-Zheng is always kind of odd because he doesn't really say what he wants, so I was a bit lost for a while. I drew all kinds of stupid things that weren't really making sense and he wasn't really giving me feedback; I think he did that intentionally... In the end he just said: "I just want you to do what you do!" From that moment on it was fine, I just got stuck in. I knew it was working when Shi-Zheng started laughing and saying how much he loved it, which was great! Then it was just the whole process of putting it together.

Originally, my starting point was the *Monkey* TV show. But during the three years of our visits to China, so many of our reference points came from what we saw during our travels. We spent a lot of money on lots of wonderful books, and we went to so many places and took thousands of photographs. I took whatever influences I'd seen in China or in the books, and just did my stuff. By the end of the second trip we came back with one song; Shi-Zheng was excited by it. By then I had met Fei Yang, who played the character Monkey. After spending time with him, eating meals and joking around, I could take some of his character – the cheekiness and playfulness – and put it into Monkey. In fact, it all goes round in circles, because he also began to take some of his character from my drawings, and eventually it all clicked into place. But I am never completely satisfied with them, even now.

For me the best memories of the project are of spending time with local people, climbing mountains; we just did so many things. We went to a monastery on top of this mountain called Monkey Mountain. When we got to the top we were above the clouds. It was like being in heaven!

Now we have 81 minutes of non-stop, in-your-face entertainment, all about Monkey, a self-important hero on a mission, with his motley crew, to redeem himself and bring holy scriptures back to China. You won't have the opportunity to get bored! There's no curtain and no pauses. We have contortionists, martial artists, animation and flying sequences. It's full on. What's next? Gorillaz are coming back...

MONKEY: JOURNEY TO THE WEST

MARK is a new design brand created to promote the growing creative renaissance that's happening in Cornwall. One of their first products is the Spin Table series, created by Tomoko Azumi to address our new, mobile lives...

Tomoko Azumi: The Spin Table is all about dealing with the mess of contemporary life. You come in from work and unload your mobile, your iPod and your digital camera from your bag or pockets, and then you have to find the chargers and plug them in. This table does it all for you nice and neatly: it's a little side table for all your mobile tools, the tools of your nomadic travelling life!

The table has a container under it to hold the extension lead and multiple plug sockets for your various transformers, adaptors and plugs. It's all stowed away out of sight. You then just put one plug in the wall socket to power them all. Sometimes you need them while they are being recharged, so I've put a handle in the top so you can just unplug the table and carry it to your bedroom or your office and plug it in again.

The trickiest thing was to make the flat-pack. It was like solving a puzzle, and it took lots of fiddling around to make it lie flat. Flat-pack was really important to reduce environmental impact and keep transport costs down. We used simple fabrication methods, using laser-cut metal that was folded and spot-welded. It assembles with one wingnut that tightens up the wooden elements, and magnets to stop the table from tipping, so you can put your wine glass or cup of tea on it safely.

The Spin Table gets its name from the spun sheet metal from which the top is made. I've tried to make the whole shape and style reflect its mobile function. Being part of the MARK co-operative is a very nice thing. They're lovely people and I really hope they do well and can sell the products.

Anna Hart: I'm an interior designer by trade and have been working in Cornwall for a number of years. I had a concept for a local furniture production project and went to see John Miller, the director of design at University College Falmouth. He had had a similar idea, so we teamed up.

There's been a creative revolution in Cornwall – it now has the highest number of art, design and media practitioners outside London.

We wanted to create a brand that promoted this new resurgence and reflected the Cornish lifestyle: relaxation and fun amidst beauty. The products are all about comfort, usability and sustainability. The name MARK suggests "trademark" and "making your mark" but also stands for Made And Realised in Kernow (the old name for Cornwall).

We approached local manufacturers to partner us and formed a design advisory panel made up of big players in the design industry to help us identify product ranges. We began commissioning work from designers around the country and launched our first range at 100% Design in 2008, with 11 different designers showing 14 products. We had great feedback on all the designs and won Best Interior Product for the Net chair by Sam Johnson. All but one of the products are now in production. In the future we hope to commission more local designers and design graduates.

The Spin Table came out of discussions within the advisory panel, who saw an opportunity for a flexible table for homes, offices and meeting rooms. So the brief to Tomoko was all about a storage solution. She's done fantastically well and it was a great privilege to work with her; her attention to detail and careful thinking through every aspect of the design is inspiring. And she has a signature style that is very well received, particularly in the Asian market.

SPIN TABLE

THE
LONDON
DESIGN
FESTIVAL

The idea of the London Design Festival is to celebrate and promote London as both the design capital of the world and the gateway to the UK's world-class creative industries. With more than 200 events each September, it needed a strong identity. I turned to Vince Frost to come up with something that would stand the test of time.

Vince Frost:
It's always exciting to be involved in the birth of a new project, and I was especially keen to take part in this because of its national and international significance; it was a real honour to be asked to do it. But it was quite a challenge to come up with something that could work to sum up shows as diverse as 100% Design, Size + Matter and Tent London.

I knew that I had to create an identity that could last, that wouldn't be tied to a particular trend and that could work as an overarching umbrella brand without diminishing the events it represented. I started by thinking about London's own identity, but quickly found it had nothing formal. So I asked myself: "What colour is London?" It is every colour, of course, but if any colour predominates, perhaps it's red, for design icons like the buses, pillar-boxes, phone boxes and the red in the Union flag.

In the creative industries people often talk about the "big D" when they want to emphasise "Design". I liked the idea of using a capital letter D to symbolise London both as the nation's capital and as the capital of British design. It even occurred to me that if the D were put on its back it would be a similar shape to a London bus. I soon saw that the D could be used across the board, from D-shaped invitations to logos on letterheads.

Having talked extensively to the design world through my work with D&AD, for whom I designed the *Ampersand* publication and annual reports, my biggest concern was to get it right not only for John Sorrell but for the design community as a whole. You just don't want to get that kind of thing wrong! I'm very pleased to see that, five years on, it's still going strong. And I'm delighted that a different designer gets to create a secondary identity to promote each year's event. The D helps endorse that work without restricting it and does the same for the design work that accompanies the hundreds of separate events.

LONDON DESIGN FESTIVAL IDENTITY

The Natural History Museum offers learning guides so that school pupils can relate exhibits in the museum to what they're learning in class. Hat-Trick Design was called in to make them easier to use.

Gareth Howat: The Natural History Museum has had learning guides for some time, but they tended to be a bit random and scrappy, often made up of poorly photocopied pages shoved into a clipboard. A few years back they used us to completely redo their identity. We came up with a more engaging, colourful approach that reflected the diversity both of the collection and of nature itself. We've designed these new learning guides to fit the new brand and be more inspirational.

There are about 14 titles in the new guides, ranging from minerals and rocks to human biology. We've worked very closely with educational writers to make sure they tied into the school coursework and were easy to read and understand. They aim to help pupils engage with the collection and really learn the stuff well.

A lot of our work went into the layout. We decided to go for a concertina format, which proved to be the easiest to use. It's now very easy to understand how the information is organised and how to fill it out.

Big efforts went into doing the cover. The old covers sent out the message that filling in the guide was like an academic test; kids would moan and groan when they were given them. So we came up with detachable covers that the pupils could play with – using them as monkey masks, or putting their fingers through to mimic animal tongues or legs. We used a white background to maintain a scientific air and reflect the branding.

It all had to be done on a pretty tight budget – 12 different titles with a print run of 5,000 for each. The biggest cost was printing but we managed to optimise the format to hit the budget.

The museum was very open-minded; it had the foresight to take a new approach and I think this has really made a difference to the way young people engage with it. At the very least they receive the workbooks in a more positive frame of mind, and they do seem to enjoy working through them.

NATURAL HISTORY MUSEUM LEARNING GUIDES

NATURAL HISTORY MUSEUM

Explore and Discover...
Animal parts
...he animal adventure

TRANSFORMATION

Thomas Heatherwick's Rolling Bridge is about transformation in two senses – it literally changes its form before your eyes, and it's also had a dramatic impact on London's Paddington Basin. Typically, it's both surprising and beautiful.

Thomas Heatherwick: The brief was to design a bridge that would open to allow a boat into a mooring on one side of the Grand Union Canal. Opening and closing bridges are a challenging thing to design because when they are in their open position, they can look like they're broken. They remind me of a picture of a footballer I once saw who had broken his leg – it was pointing at an angle that you didn't want to see... I wanted to make a bridge that looked like a complete object when it was open as well as when it was closed; that, as it got out of the way for a boat, would transform, rather than dislocate and break.

I had started thinking about Jim Henson puppet animatronics where the mechanisms are concealed within a rubber skin, but I realised that a rubber bridge was too interesting – it would be better if it looked more unassuming before it moved. We thought that, in its closed position, it should appear calm and unobtrusive, not really giving much of a clue about how it would open.

It was from these thoughts that the idea of a bridge that rolls up came about. One end starts to lift and the bridge curls upwards and backwards, its furthest ends kissing each other, forming an octagon. You can see the hydraulic rams in the balustrade, but I find that no one says to me, "Ah yes, I can see what that's going to do!" even though its mechanism is visible. We worked with engineers SKM Anthony Hunts, together with Primary Fluid Power and Solent Fluid Power, as well as DJW Consulting and steel constructors Littlehampton Welding. It was this team that really made the Rolling Bridge happen.

Tourists started turning up in Paddington Basin to watch it; as it only opened when a boat wanted to come through, they often had a long wait. So, to satisfy the visitors, it now opens at midday every Friday.

PADDINGTON BASIN ROLLING BRIDGE

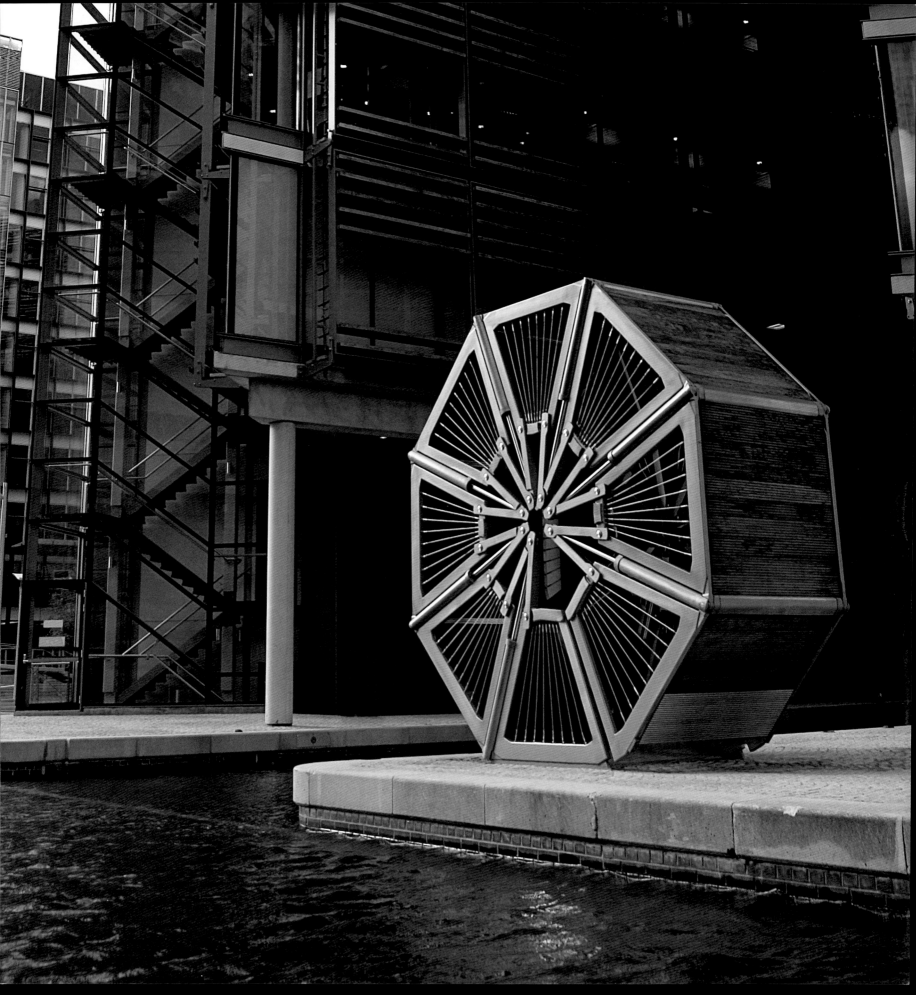

Among his many other projects, Martino Gamper collects old, broken chairs. He had so many that he decided it was time to do something with them. So he challenged himself to make them into 100 chairs – and to do it at the rate of a chair a day.

Martino Gamper: I've been collecting half-broken bits of chairs from the streets of London for years. It was partly about reappropriating ideas, finding the value in something that someone else had thrown away. Perhaps I could take them apart and build new chairs from the broken bits. So I started collecting more and more, finding them all over London, on the streets, on wasteland... I bought a few from junk shops and boot sales for around £5. Some were given by friends who had heard that I was looking for them. Ron Arad gave me an Arne Jacobsen chair – he'd had some in his house and this one was broken.

A few years earlier in 2003 I was asked by Janice Blackburn of Sotheby's if I could make some chairs for an exhibition called *Waste to Taste*. I realised that to really make an impact I needed more than the ten pieces she'd asked for. So I decided to give myself the constraint that, every day, I should make one chair.

The process was fascinating. I learnt a lot about how they're made and how they can be reassembled. I also began to understand the character of chairs, and I tried to make each one an individual character. I loved the instant process. I didn't have to sketch or draw, or make 2D and 3D models. I just wrestled with the various bits and made instant objects. I tried to pretend it was an industrial project; perhaps I could find one or two that could potentially be produced commercially... Each one has a story for me, about where I found it, what state it was in, what it reminded me of. I found a Vespa seat. Vespa motorbikes featured a lot in my early youth; they were the bikes that everyone young in Italy wanted to have. It was great to find it lying there on the side of the road in Victoria Park in East London. Amazing! Impossible! So far away from home... I called the finished chair the Vespino.

The idea was that people could sit down on some strange creations that offer unexpected comfort. The chairs are now touring in Europe.

100 DAYS/100 CHAIRS

Switched On London is a lighting festival that showcases sustainable lighting design in the night-time urban environment. It commissioned Jason Bruges to do something special with London Bridge.

Jason Bruges:
I'm fascinated by the relationship that people have with their environment and I love to get them to engage with it. In an age of iPods and mobile phones, all too often people walk through their world barely noticing it exists; so you'll understand that we do a lot of work involving pedestrians.

We were given the east side of London Bridge to work with. We created a programmable line of coloured light that ran parallel to the balustrade. The idea was to illustrate the daily tidal flow of commuters across the river. The animation of this piece was about the speed people walk, their gait, where they pause. The lights moving along the bridge indicated what the pedestrians were actually doing, but on a larger scale. We even tried to influence them: we'd speed the animation up or slow it down to see if they changed pace.

We could pick on a single person, match their walking speed and then slowly try to coax them into speeding up. Some reacted, and some, of course, simply didn't notice. Some would smile as they got the joke, others actually played and danced with the lights! And some were confused; we'd housed the lighting in the handrail, so quite a number of people couldn't tell where the light was coming from – they were looking up at the sky for some sort of projection unit.

We've done a number of pieces with a similar feel. We did one on a Richard Rogers building in Broad Street which recorded the movement of the external lifts, and then played back a lighting sequence in the lift shaft when the building was empty. Another project, *Wind and Light*, at the Queen Elizabeth Hall on the South Bank, included an array of micro-wind turbines arranged on the roof. The turbines would turn in sequence as the wind blew so you could track the air as it moved over the roof. We're currently working on a piece in London's Ropemaker Street. It's a chandelier hanging in a vertical air duct which literally scavenges energy from the airflow...

NORTH-SOUTH OVER EAST-WEST

I saw WEmake's Street Sofa, made from a wheelie bin, at the Laban exhibition and bought it on the spot. Later I asked WEmake to make me a Wheelie Bin Desk. They are immensely creative and take recycling to its logical conclusion.

Jason Allcorn: It all came from DD04 (Deptford Design04), part of the London Design Festival. They called on designers to contribute to an exhibition and gave each of us a standard Eurobin – the sort of wheelie bin you see outside pubs and shops for rubbish and recycling. The brief was, effectively, "be creative...".

WEmake is all about giving waste a new lease of life. We like to try to get people thinking beyond just putting bottles in a bottlebank. With a bit of alteration, waste products can look pretty good even alongside modern style icons, telling their old story as well as a brand new one. We sat down and thought: "What can we do with a dead dustbin?" These bins are on almost every city street corner, so we decided to turn ours into a Street Sofa.

That led to a commission to build an office desk. It's made from the smaller 660 litre Eurobin, and it was a lot more difficult than the Street Sofa. It's mainly made up of bits of the chopped-up bin painstakingly cut and welded back together. The drawers were especially difficult; we wanted them to work smoothly. Welding thin galvanised steel to the necessary tolerances took some practice. We lined them in reclaimed wood and adapted a locking system from an old filing cabinet.

The top of the bin is a sheet of sustainable (FSC) plywood with a steel band around the lip, securing a large leather panel. I'd like to say I'd found the leather in a skip too, but no, the client wanted the perfect writing surface...

WHEELIE BIN DESK

Mozart's La Clemenza di Tito *is a story about a Roman emperor who learns understanding and mercy. Es Devlin designed her remarkable sets for the opera around the themes of hierarchy, destruction and rebirth.*

Es Devlin: The initial conversation between a director and a designer is often all about instincts: you listen to the piece you're going to work on, and then you come to each other with your visions. During our first meeting on this project, Francisco Negrín told me he saw it all happening on a skyscraper, with the drama's high point being some terrible accident like *The Towering Inferno* (in the opera, Vesuvius erupts at the end of the first act). It was a compelling vision.

I then spent several months listening to the opera and learning about the era of the Austrian Enlightenment, and, of course, the Roman Empire. The more I studied, the less I could find a way in the music to accommodate the skyscraper concept. *Clemenza di Tito* contains some of the most exquisite music ever written, but it's been roundly criticised for being old-fashioned, as if Mozart had abandoned experimentation for established form. Indeed, *Clemenza* employs a long-established structure to deliver *opera seria* – serious opera, with a message – Tito (the emperor Titus) moves from tyranny towards clemency, and his eventual wife, Vitellia, moves from foolishness to enlightenment. It was, to me, about the conflict of

hierarchy, the battle between tyranny and democracy. And out of all this immersive study arose floor plans from the destruction of Pompeii.

I took ground plans of high-status Pompeiian architecture, and flipped them up so that they became like a front elevation. The audience first sees this ground plan as if it's been hung on a wall. When the screen rises, you can see the ground plan has been extruded into a structure, with the characters walking around it as if they're negotiating the storeys of a vertical building. They are, if you like, the hierarchical structures of human life, all created in the shadow of the great natural force, Mount Vesuvius.

In Act 2, after the eruption, the vertical structure has fallen down and it's literally back to the drawing-board, a return to the ground plan. Like a ghost town, all the structures are covered in ash. And, as Tito and Vitellia make their personal transitions, the ruins begin to emerge from the ash, full of light, vigour, green shoots and new beginnings.

I'm not exactly sure how I came up with the idea of an extruded ground plan; if it sounds mysterious, it's because it is mysterious, like listening to music is mysterious. That's one of the great joys of listening to great music – it's beyond words; you can't really describe your responses. It's that magic that has led me to concentrate on design for opera and pop; I love music's curious ability to bypass the rational mind. I love the direct conversation between music and image that somehow leaves brute logic out of the dialogue.

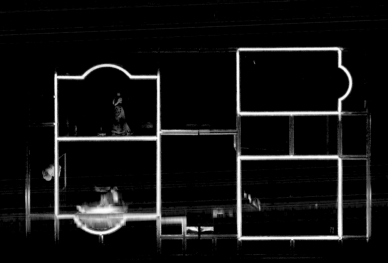

The British Council invited artist Chris Ofili to represent Britain at the 50th Venice Biennale. He contacted architect David Adjaye and structural engineers Ove Arup, and, in a complex collaboration, created a stunning environment of paint and glass, light and colour, in which to house his exhibition Within Reach.

Chris Ofili: My first thoughts were that I probably shouldn't do this exhibition at all. I hadn't really planned to go into another year of working so intensely and was actually intending to have a gap year during this time. But I went along to see the space and the first thing I did was to look up. I immediately became aware of the light source coming from above and felt a connection between what I was seeing and some of the paintings that I was doing at the time that featured an overhanging light, or energy source. This got me excited about what I could do. I started to talk to David Adjaye about the space. Because David had studied architecture he had a better understanding of things that I may have had just a feeling about, but that he could articulate.

Red, green and black relate to ideas that Marcus Garvey had in the 1920s about African people all round the world. The red signified the blood that had been shed by people of African descent for the green of the land that was being fought over, and the black signified the beautiful skin of the people. He used these colours to create a pan-African flag to unify all African people. It was about Afro pride, but I also see it as a way of presenting Afro unity in a more romantic sense. I think Garvey saw Africa as a place of paradise, a place to be happy. I think that's a beautiful idea, a wonderfully unifying and relaxing ideal.

The kaleidoscope in the main space, and the rooms around it, were a way for the viewer to always feel immersed in this red, black and greenness. My paintings signify love and unity and romance and togetherness. They're essentially about being happy and are often linked with ideas of paradise and spiritual contentment; though some contain elements that threaten that equilibrium. But I don't evaluate my pictures too much – if I do, it suggests closure, and I don't like closure...

David Adjaye: My involvement came out of collaborating with Chris on a work called *The Upper Room* at Victoria Miro Gallery, London, which is now in the Tate collection. The concept was to make a room specifically designed to complement Chris's paintings, to use architecture to help the visitors really engage with them. In Venice we proposed to go a step further: we'd use the architecture to bring the audience right inside the paintings themselves.

My job was to conceal the Palladian architecture of the Venice pavilion and bring forth specific proportions and spaces to the service of the paintings. We created pure colour fields in each room, with floors, walls and ceilings done in red, green and black. We put felt on the walls and carpeted the floors to create what was, effectively, a series of acoustic wombs. The idea was to dematerialise the three-dimensionality of the rooms and make 2D picture plains. Each room was painted and lit accordingly: you might enter a colour field of red to view a green painting, you might look from a green colour field into a red room.

The centrepiece was the shingle glass dome. We wanted to flip people's expected reading of this entrance space, so we created a dome within a dome to force people to walk round a corridor made by the wall between the outer original dome and the inner one we had created. At the centre was a solar celestial body suspended in space and emanating radial light, based on a painting of a seven-pointed star by Chris. Arup were brought on board to come up with a way of translating his work into 200 suspended glass tiles, each covered in a black, red or green film, all apparently bursting from the central disk, with no apparent fixings; a drawing made in glass. It looked as if the light source was emitting a shower of sharp glass that was falling down into the main space – it was quite disconcerting! You looked up and saw yourself refracted amid the kaleidoscopic imagery; you gazed up at the shards and became part of the work.

It was only at the end that we realised how extraordinarily hard it had been for Arup to build it. The incredible network of trusses and beams supporting the 200 pieces of glass in apparently effortless suspension is permanently etched in my mind!

BRITISH PAVILION VENICE BIENNALE

In London's Soho there is a restaurant where the menus appear to be part of the table – you simply choose and touch, and the order goes through to the kitchen. It's just part of the magic created by Blacksheep.

Tim Mutton: The brief was built around the idea of having an interactive restaurant with menus delivered through a projection unit right on to the tables themselves. The idea was to be able to book everything from your starter to a taxi just by touching items projected on to the table . We were working for entrepreneurs Danny Potter and Noel Hunwick; they wanted the restaurant to be warm and theatrical in contrast to the stark and clinical decors that have been so popular recently, and which might have been expected from such a technology-led restaurant.

We opted for a kaleidoscopic theme in the decor, which seemed to go with the projections; diners can even choose their own virtual tablecloth for their tables. But we didn't want to overdo it and turn it into some "multi-coloured swap shop". So we kept most of the walls relatively simple, using an off-white wallpaper with a slight sparkle in it and making large graphics, the appearance of which changes according to the intensity of the lighting.

There were plenty of technical issues to be sorted; not many restaurants have a computer server room! It felt like designing for a jumbo jet – we'd never packed so much equipment and cabling into a restaurant's ceiling space before. We had to create bespoke fibreglass "drums" to cover the 30 projection units, all easily removable for maintenance. The projectors throw off a lot of heat, so we had to deal with that too. The tables use track pads to link your finger movements to the software, and they all required battery packs that had to be accommodated. We had to fit all this, plus space for 70 covers, into a smallish property on Wardour Street. We even had to build an extension out the back.

It was a fascinating project; we think we've managed to create a sensuous, social space with a strong personality to balance the technology. This project follows a series of high-profile bars and clubs we've designed in London; we love working with entrepreneurial clients; it's always demanding, but usually highly creative.

INAMO RESTAURANT

Hussein Chalayan created the Motion Dress series to point to the future of fashion design. He's determined to turn these brilliant ideas into commercial reality.

Hussein Chalayan: The idea here was to reflect how dresses have changed over the years, and how their shapes have been influenced and informed; why we dress in certain ways in one era and other ways in another. So I've tried to capture these changes in dresses that can transform their shape to suit a series of 20th-century styles. The earlier shapes are a bit more body-shy, and the skirt gets bigger as the era goes on before it collapses and gets smaller and less "waisted" for the '60s. In the 2007 show, a sheer white dress wound itself up into a hat, leaving the model completely nude…

Of course, this couldn't be all my own work – I don't have the technical expertise. There were many people involved, including a prototyping company, an electrical engineer, a mechanical engineer; Moritz Waldemeyer did some brilliant computer programming. It was a bit like making a car.

I don't yet have the resources to make such dresses commercially available, so they're prototypes. But the intention is to make them real. There are many problems to solve – how can you clean them, what happens if the power fails, how can you sit down in them? The pictured dress is an extreme example, but others are softer, with corsets designed to hold all the technology to control the dress.

Of course it will be easier in the future, but why not take the steps toward it anyway? I don't want to abandon these ideas; this is not about momentary achievements that create excitement and are then forgotten, these dresses look forward. I believe they can be achieved. The plan is to persuade companies to collaborate, but in the current climate that's super-difficult; understandably, they want to see dollar signs at the end!

It's great when people are excited about your work, but you must be excited yourself. You want to share your work and hope people will be inspired by it, but, of course, it can be frustrating; people do have expectations and they can't always be realised. The key is to have belief in yourself.

THE MOTION DRESS SERIES

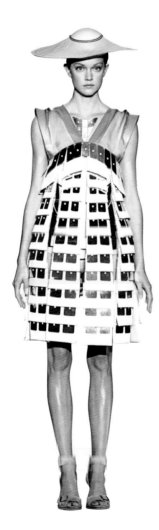

Brett Foraker is the creative director of Channel 4. His team wanted to create a new visual identity that reflected the channel's high production values, multicultural remit, constant evolution and wit.

Brett Foraker: We knew we needed to freshen up the brand, but we didn't know quite how or what shape it should take. We engaged some design agencies but when they sent in their ideas we didn't feel particularly inspired. In the meantime we'd been working with the Moving Picture Company on the E4 identity and I had collaborated with their 3D designer/ director Russell Appleford. I did some DV film tests and Russell flew in some animation, and we realised we had the basis of what we were looking for: a slow reveal of the C4 logo emerging from the scenery we had shot.

Traditionally, logos really make sure you know they are there. But we worked to a different principle: in every ident the logo resolves for *only one frame* and each time you spot it, it feels like a little reward.

Music was key. I'd sit with Richard Martin, a genius musician, and listen to music we liked, or that we found tonally interesting, and then we'd select material that would inform the films. One of my favourites is for the Dubai ident. We shot the waterfront from a helicopter, panning round in a wide sweep to reveal the logo made up of half-built skyscrapers. We've kept the helicopter wash in the top of shot (which is usually edited out) and edited in the shadow of the helicopter on the buildings at the start of the film, marking the ones that would become the logo. Richard Martin mixed the percussive helicopter sound with Arabic

music and keyboard arpeggio to create an expectant, driving crescendo.

In the Tokyo street scene there's a nice piece of misdirection. You are walking down the street following a bicycle that turns right. From a shop on your right comes a burst of female pop music – the stores in Japan have their own sonic identities and we wanted to reflect what it sounds like to be walking down a Tokyo street. You watch the cyclist disappear, your eyes follow a hooded walker turning left and then you focus on the big red neon sign hanging in front of you. You turn round, walking sideways and backwards, to see the C4 logo behind you. The logo, present from frame 1, had been assembling in the mid- and background.

Channel 4's remit is to be gritty, so some of these are filmed in the last places you'd expect, like on a motorway with some insane driver cutting you up to get to the sliproad, or the rainswept balcony of a council estate... We want to show beauty in texture and form where you're not used to seeing it.

The films generally take a day to shoot and then several months in post-production. Russell Appleford and his team created wire frame models of each of the blocks making up the 4's characters. He then rendered and textured the blocks to suit the film's environment. Lead operator Mark Stannard painstakingly matched the blocks to the live-action background plates, and, once the blocks were positioned correctly, we honed the textures and lighting. The earlier executions, like the pylons (shot from a moving car) don't look physically possible. For the later ones we thought: if we're spending all this time trying to make everything appear as real as possible, we should make the logo actually look like it was a believable accident of the landscape...

FLUIDITY

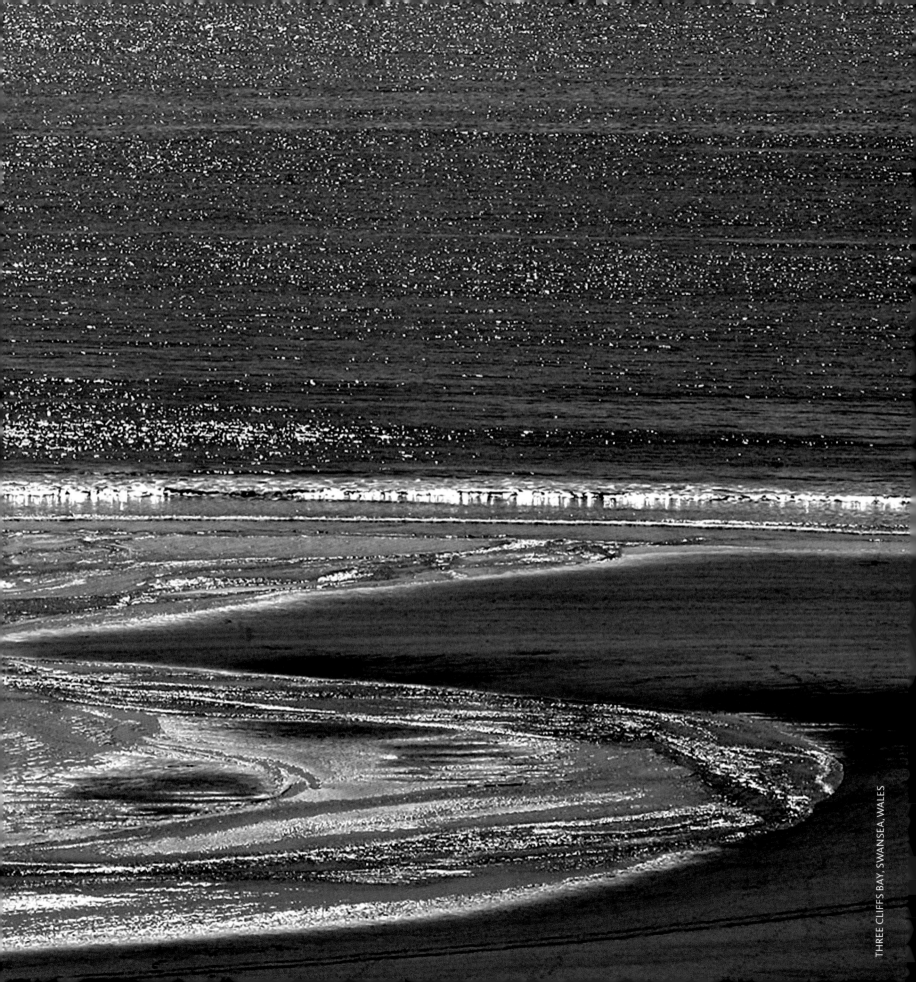

Welsh-born designer Ross Lovegrove was commissioned by Ty Nant to create a new recyclable water bottle. His solution captures the essence of fluidity.

Ross Lovegrove:
Ty Nant wanted me to design a PET [polyethylene terephthalate] bottle (PET is relatively easy to recycle) and they wanted me to colour it with their famous blue. I spent three months on it, researching all types of possibilities, including crushable bottles and using less material… I realised that everything I was doing was just an industrial solution. Most water bottles look like they're designed for factory, transportation and for stacking on shelves in a supermarket. None of the brands I looked at attempted to project the concept of water. I found myself thinking more and more about what water means. We're in an age in which no one should own water and sell it; it's about survival; it should be free for everyone in the world. And as for bottles – clouds and pipes carry water much more efficiently.

After three months of thinking like this, I intellectualised myself out of a job; I called the client and offered to give them their money back, saying that I'd failed and was embarrassed at being drawn into something I didn't believe in. The chief executive said:

"Calm down! Take your time and talk it through – we really want you to do this."

Then I was ill – my immune system crashed – and I went to Thailand to recover. I took a book on the water studies of Leonardo da Vinci: incredible work. Water is so hard to capture; you look down, draw, and when you look back up, it's changed. Da Vinci's work was, really, the first impressionism. I found myself warming to the challenge again. I tried to create a surface that presented the essence of water, that captures its impression, something beyond the commercial, a gesture towards the iconography of water itself. I dropped the blue, which isn't the colour of water as we see it and is harder to recycle. I did an exercise in the studio – how long would it take to design a standard water bottle, a rotational shape, coloured blue? It took nine minutes. Mine took me the best part of 14 months.

But I knew that, at the end of the day, it was just about blowing a balloon of PET into a mould and I told my client that I'd find someone who could do it; it didn't take long to find an English manufacturer.

The response has been astonishing. Some people have described it as "affordable, accessible art, the solidification of fluidity". But I have to thank Ty Nant for bearing with me; they're a fantastic client.

TY NANT WATER BOTTLE

The fluidity of Universal Everything's work for Audi captures the spirit and feel of a brand-new model of car, without ever showing the car itself.

Matt Pyke: Ten artists were invited to create a high-performance artwork that reflected in some way the new shape and form of the latest Audi TT car. The artists ranged from ourselves to a poet and a ballet company. The idea was to exhibit the art at a gallery in Sydney, Australia.

The openness of the brief was really appealing; Audi gave us only the shape of the car to work with – we had no details at all. We started research and found ourselves attracted to the industry's scientific imagery. Wind-tunnel images intrigued us especially; they had a beauty that appealed to both the artists and the engineers in us. And so was born the idea of using a wind-tunnel effect to "paint" the car and define its silhouette.

Originally we had the idea of using a 3D animation program to create the wind-tunnel, but had to abandon it – it was too complex mathematically to simulate wind. So we went another way, working with programmer Karsten Schmidt to create some original visual software that could generate flowing coloured lines that would move over the shape of the car. They captured the "carness" of the Audi without actually showing any detail of the car itself. It was almost like a tease campaign...

It's an extremely ambient piece of advertising; a dynamic painting that reveals the car's shape. The performance went down very well and attracted the attention of Audi's ad agency in Canada, Lowe Roche. They took the idea and projected it on to motorway tunnels and skyscrapers throughout Toronto.

AUDI TT VIRAL VIDEO

New technologies will make it possible to have animated wallpaper that changes its design by the day, or, indeed, the minute. Daniel Brown is a pioneer in this field, creating truly mesmeric images.

 Daniel Brown: My first version of Interactive Flowers was just an on-line demonstration of real-time fractals [self-generating patterns and images guided by mathematical formulae] that was very much a technical experiment. It's a simple idea; you watch flowers develop and grow all over your computer screen. I put them on the web and they were immediately popular, which, to be honest, was a bit of a shock. I wasn't expecting non-technical people to like them, but they loved the organic aesthetic. My work caught a wave; partly because my website was one of the first to use new Flash and Shockwave software, so publicity quickly followed.

I've steadily been improving the flowers at the same time as working on other projects. My company's called Play-Create, and we create "Software as Furniture" – moving, decorative imagery in the home.

My Eureka moment came when I realised that if I had a white room, with everything white – walls, ceilings, floor, tables, chairs, cutlery, plates – then it could become anything I wanted; I could have never-ending variations projected on all surfaces. The key is new projector technology coupled with digital paper and new flat-screen systems. Soon it will be possible to have entire walls capable of offering the most beautiful images, animations and scenery.

I think I'm among the first of a generation who honestly can't be sure whether they are computer programmers or designers... My work comes out of my computer programming background; for me mathematics is the language of nature.

I'm currently looking at designing new digital species of flowers, custom-made for clients. They will grow on screen and be exclusively yours.

INTERACTIVE FLOWERS

The new €1 billion terminal at Barajas Airport aims to establish Madrid as a major European hub. Rogers Stirk Harbour + Partners wanted to make sure it worked well on the human scale.

Ivan Harbour:
The Barajas building is 1.2 kilometres long, more than a million square metres, a real megastructure. It's a microcosm of a city intended to handle some 50 million people a year. How do you humanise something on such a vast scale? The corporate colour-decision reaction is typically a clinical grey, silver or white, but we suggested a wide range of colours so that people could find their way. The building was too vast to be considered as a single designed entity, so we chose to design it as the ultimate kit of parts, with the smallest pieces designed at a human scale and their forms repeating to create the whole.

The drama comes from making adjustments to the spatial relationship between those components. We were committed to using the best sustainable materials and we wanted to make sure the energy systems were really efficient, working passively to cool the building, despite the soaring Madrid temperatures.

The realisation is the part I enjoy most about architecture, and it's great just to have been part of getting such a monumental project built! Once it's finished, there's both depression and joy. The depression comes from seeing the bits that most people don't notice – the few bits that you couldn't resolve quite as you wanted. The joy comes from watching people react to what you've done.

One of the best moments was watching a rowdy bunch of Arsenal supporters come into the building: they stopped, went quiet and just looked up...

Richard Rogers:
The spur for our thinking behind Barajas was the pure excitement of travel. I remember going to Paris after the war and seeing trains headed for Istanbul; standing in a great station and looking up at the boards displaying such romantic destinations – it just lifts the soul! It's the sort of feeling you get in the best Victorian railway stations, but airports tend to lack that special magic, that sense of the spirit of the voyage.

The central concept was to bring natural light into as much of the building as possible. So we designed the roof in a waveform, the crests of which accommodated large windows that brought the sun streaming down, via canyons of light, into the lower parts of the building. The bamboo cladding really accentuates the shape of the wave, which, to my mind, harks back to those Brunel railway stations of 150 years ago, with their magnificent arched glass roofs. We had a terrific client and enjoyed a great relationship; they had plenty of questions but we always worked together creatively. It took about six years to build, which, compared to Heathrow's Terminal 5, was pretty quick! The main terminal is nearly a kilometre long, so we decided to use a rainbow of colours to give it identity. It meant people could say, "Meet me at Gate 66, where it's all pink...".

BARAJAS AIRPORT

Keira Knightley's dress in Atonement *wowed the critics. It was designed by Jacqueline Durran, who won an Oscar nomination for her work on the 2005 film version of* Pride and Prejudice.

Jacqueline Durran: Costume design for film is distinct from other kinds of clothes design – it's all about the brief. I always want as much information as possible about what we want to achieve. It's like a conundrum that I have to solve to bring it all together. Film costumes are usually representative of either the character or a mood or a combination of the two. In *Atonement* Keira Knightley's character, Cecilia Tallis, was a slightly idle, upper-class woman of the middle 1930s. Joe Wright [the director] wanted to encapsulate the searing heat of a hot summer's day, so Cecilia's dress had to be as light, airy, transparent and representative of heat as we could make it. That was the main brief. My starting point was to combine a 1930s evening dress with the idea that the hot day would move into a sultry evening.

I gathered as much reference material as I could, spending days trawling through copies of *Vogue* from the 1930s and books on late '20s and early '30s eveningwear. I was especially inspired by the French designer Madeleine Vionnet and the photographs of Jacques Henri Lartigue and Antoinette Frissell. I didn't want to be slavishly accurate to the period; it was more about the spirit of the '30s infused with the '70s to be appealing to the modern eye.

When you're designing for a film the first thing you do is employ a cutter. Their brief is often to make the costume sufficiently robust for the rigours of filming. In this instance the dress had to be feather-light, so I employed Jo Van Schuppen, who cuts for Vivienne Westwood, and who trained in fashion rather than film. The lightness of the dress meant we had to make about ten of them, knowing that the material might rip in the passionate embrace in the steamy library scene (it did!). Joe told me that he would be shooting the movement of the dress's hemline, so I gave the hem a greater diameter than was historically accurate, to lend it more flow as Keira walked. I wanted to get the top half of the dress to have a "naked" feel, to suggest that if Keira turned quickly she might actually pop out of it. I wanted it to feel like she was hardly inside it, so the bodice wasn't tight but had some volume away from the body to increase the feeling of nudity. It reminded me of being a child and wearing a hood; you turn your head but the hood stays looking forward.

We made a silk band that wrapped round the upper hips in a late-'20s style. The bow detail was inspired by a Lartigue photo of a satin dress, but instead of adding a beading to the edge, we cut it with a laser, which provides a clean edge without loose fibres. The two tails of the bow dropped down either side of the front split, partly masking it. The design was guided by minimalism – we were always trying to take stuff away. Looking back, my favourite elements were the way that the fabric twisted into the shoulder and the faux detail in the front.

Finding the perfect emerald green wasn't easy. We went to one of the silk houses in London and asked them to pull out samples of greens in a range of cloths. We then piled them up alongside each other and came up with a combination of a lime-green silk, a black and green organza and a green chiffon. We looked at the combination and thought, "God, that's beautiful!" I then called master dyer Tim Shanahan and asked him to buy 100 yards of plain white satin chiffon and try to recreate the colour from a combination of the three hues. That's an incredibly hard thing to do, but, happily, the guy's a genius, and he pulled it off.

So this dress wasn't my work alone, it was a dream combination of elements. I might have made the same dress, but if the director hadn't shot it so well, or the lighting hadn't been so brilliant, or if Keira hadn't been looking more beautiful than she ever had before, it wouldn't have been as powerful. It was a collaboration and I think that all these elements came together to make the impact the dress has made.

CECILIA'S DRESS IN ATONEMENT

Kew Gardens wanted to attract visitors into the centre of the garden. They turned to John Pawson to design them a minimalist bridge which was not just about getting from one side of the lake to the other.

John Pawson: I met Lucy Blythe, the fundraiser for Kew, during a party at the V&A and she told me about a plan to encourage people to use the middle of Kew Gardens. She described a pathway, like an arc, cutting through the lake, which would help draw people further in. She said they needed a footbridge or people were going to get very wet, and told me Kew had received some good architectural ideas but they all had problems with either being too much of a statement or too expensive, or both. So it was music to her ears when I told her I was a minimalist.

The man in charge of the trees at Kew is Tony Kirkham and he's the man. He told me he wanted something that would fit with the trees and the plants, and he said it would be good if the lake crossing were not just about getting from one side to the other, but was an experience in itself.

I started thinking of traditional Japanese or Chinese bridges. I considered stepping stones, like the granite ones you find on Exmoor, but Health and Safety put an end to that – apparently you can't have people falling in any more. I even thought of a sunken pathway, like some sort of glass-walled Red Sea Crossing. In the end I realised that they wanted something that just skimmed over the water, that was just high enough for the ducks to get under; but which had as little visible support as possible.

Buro Happold did a great job of hiding the support. What you don't see is the steel outriggers under the bridge. They support rails upon which lie the granite sleepers that make up the walkway – they rise up to form the separated balusters. It's a bit like a railway track upside down.

I picked two colours from the garden; a leafy gold reflected in the bronze balusters, and the shadowy grey of the granite, reflecting shaded tree trunks. The serpentine shape came about because the bridge had to spring from the bank and move towards an island before picking up the path on the other side. It reflects the gently rounded shoreline and the natural contours of its setting. The night lighting, LEDs between each baluster, was an afterthought. It occurred to me that they were promoting late-night opening so they'd need the bridge illuminated. They agreed, but still wanted to bring the project in at under a million pounds. I worked hard with Speirs & Major Lighting to get the lights done for less than £100,000.

I like the fact that the bridge is so animated; you've got the moving water underneath, the wildlife and the people. I love seeing people hypnotised by the reflection of the moving water in the golden balusters; I love seeing them enjoying being on it, lingering on it, trying to play the balusters like a xylophone…

The crossing was created by teamwork, really. My role, when fellow designers and engineers had made their vital points, was to have the final say and ensure that it happened.

SACKLER CROSSING AT KEW GARDENS

When William Murray Hamm got the opportunity to work to a brief that they helped write themselves, it's no surprise it was all about creativity. They came up with an award-winning concept for direct marketing.

Richard Murray: A former blue chip client of ours, Cees van de Water, told us he'd decided to set up his own marketing consultancy. His aim was to help retailers unlock their brand potential through creativity by identifying opportunities and consumer trends, and assisting during agency selection, brand development and implementation.

We suggested it was a good chance to create a new, innovative identity. Cees really enjoys creative design work so we saw an opportunity to push the boundaries a little. We sat down and wrote a brief with him. Creativity was the start point; releasing creative potential. The best idea that emerged from the subsequent brainstorms was chromatography, the idea that if you put treated paper in water it can create random colours; it works a bit like litmus paper. It also worked rather well with his surname!

Chromatographic paper is not new; this could have been done any time over the last 50 years or more, but this application is novel. Creativity often involves putting something old in a new environment and giving it a twist that makes it appear fresh in a specific context.

The idea is that the stationery and mailshots become interactive. Business cards or promotional leaflets carry the instruction to "dip in water". When you do, the coloured designs appear, literally releasing their creativity in front of your eyes. Sometimes important text will only appear when you get it wet – it's like secret writing. How much it changes and colours depends on how much water you use and how long you soak it for, so it's personalised, in a curious sort of way. The intensity of the colours is unique to each circumstance.

The designs animate nicely on the website, so it works well in the digital arena too. Cees has had a lot of positive feedback. His clients love the novelty of it, saying it commands attention and provokes response. The idea says a lot about Cees's company: that it's deliberately provocative and inventive, and that, as a potential client, you can see them showing similar creativity when they work for you.

Design doesn't need to be complicated. This tells a simple story with a simple solution. Good work often comes from a tight brief; had it been more open, it would have been much harder, but a specific starting point will usually force you to respond in the best way.

WATER-BRANDING IDENTITY

Longchamp, a French producer of handbags, leather goods and luggage, commissioned Heatherwick Studio to design its new flagship store in New York's SoHo district. Its centrepiece – a 60 ton steel "landscape" staircase – is widely considered to be a work of art.

Thomas Heatherwick:
We designed a bag for Longchamp a few years ago. At the time, our studio was near a zip factory and we became interested in the fact that zip is manufactured and sold in lengths of 200 metres – how could anyone need a zip that long? We began experimenting with these long pieces of zip – making objects, dresses and accessories. The experiments developed into a new kind of expanding bag – the Zip Bag – which became a best-seller. A year after the launch, Jean Cassegrain, the managing director of Longchamp, called me and asked if we would be interested in designing their New York flagship store. They had taken a building in SoHo which they wanted to develop as their hundredth store, the largest to date. He said they would send through an image of the site.

When the pictures turned up, we saw a rather strange, uncharacteristic building with a number of rather permanent-looking shops inside. We spoke to Jean and asked when the retailers of the ground floor were moving out. He told us they were staying – Longchamp were using the large space on the first floor, with only a small entrance at street level. In retail, our understanding is that the ground floor is king, as that's where most customers prefer to stay, so we had a challenge: how were we going to get people to walk off the pavement and lift their bodies to a floor above without feeling like it was too much effort?

If you're going to make someone walk upstairs it needs to be a very special place when they arrive, and we wanted the sales floor to feel generous. So we proposed to build another floor on top of the building. That way, we could maximise the space and build a Longchamp world up there where the Cassegrain family could meet clients and buyers and hold events. We cut a huge hole through the two floors of the building to bring daylight down and to help draw people upwards. We then knew we had to make the most un-staircase-like staircase that we could.

The result is more of a landscape to pull you upwards. The idea of using steel ribbons came because we needed to connect the street level to the main space on the second floor. The stair landscape uses 60 tons of steel strips to make a cascade of ribbons lined with a raw natural-coloured rubber. Because there is so much steel, we used magnets to attach the bags and lights. We also designed special tripod objects to display the bags – that look like gremlin skiers sliding down the staircase…

We worked very closely with the Cassegrain family. Jean came to almost every meeting, whether it was London or New York or Paris. He knows where every screw and fixing is – that's the reason why the project worked so well.

LA MAISON UNIQUE FOR LONGCHAMP

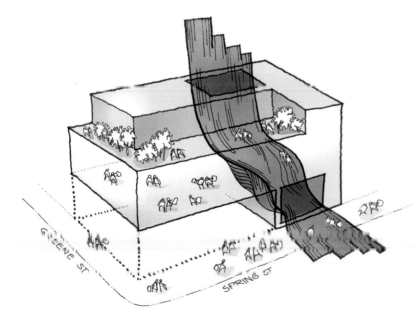

Designing a set of domestic balance scales might seem like reinventing the wheel, but, using new technologies, Sebastian Conran found plenty of room for innovation. His inspiration? A walk on one of England's most famous beaches...

Sebastian Conran: I was approached by Bliss Homeware who told me that they thought there was a market for kitchen balance scales. Since digital models had come along, there were no modern balance scales to be had. The following weekend, after a brainstorming session with Mike Schneideman from Divertimenti, I was in Dorset strolling out along the magnificent Chesil Beach. Chesil is remarkable for its egg-like pebbles, graded by nature into different sizes. I was about to throw a pebble into the sea, when I felt its weight in my hand. I thought – these would make perfect kitchen scale weights.

I hoped we could use natural stones, but quickly realised that, for accuracy, we'd have to manufacture them. I started a dialogue with the prospective manufacturer, Hong Kong-based Alex Wong, and soon we were discussing using die-cast zinc. We used new software that allowed us to design an ovoid shape to an exact weight.

In the meantime Mike and I were working on the scales themselves. Cleanliness was a big issue; traditional scales collect greasy kitchen dirt, so we made sure all the surfaces, inside and out, were wipe-clean. We made the trays out of translucent blue plastic, partly in response to the fashion created by the Blueberry iMac computer. And, working with design colleague Joanne Hargreaves, we used laser-cut folded stainless steel for the internal balance mechanism, which made it much easier to manufacture.

A buzz built up around the product immediately after launch. At John Lewis we noticed a curious thing – the weights were outselling the scales. We watched customers spot the shiny weights, pick one up, fondle it and then make the decision to buy. It made me think of a great test for successful design – the blind test. If your product works for people just by feel, it's a good indicator that you've got the whole design right. I must confess I'm very proud of the scales; it's led to a whole range of kitchenware products.

EQUILIBRIUM SCALES

Around the Corner was Amanda Levete's first solo exhibition. It was presented by Established & Sons, for whom she had previously designed two best-selling products, the Chester sofa and the Drift series.

Amanda Levete: This show was about using furniture to explore spatial relationships in a corner. Corners are often neglected spaces. In our architectural work at Future Systems, corners are noticeable by their absence, so this show was a little ironic. *Around the Corner* was about showing how the space that frames a corner can become as important as the piece itself; how the void is as important as the solid. So these four pieces were part experiment and part space solution.

Each piece looked to push the boundaries of what materials could do and how their properties affect their function. North is a console in neon fibreglass, East is a desk carved from a single piece of black marble, South is a set of two shelves in Corian (a plastic developed by DuPont) and West (pictured) is a sinuous bench made from laminated wood. We used digital technology to cut and carve the forms, and the pieces were finished off by hand.

I wanted to show how you could evolve a design language to respond to the material. The fluid, twisting forms in these pieces have consequently influenced some of the buildings we're designing. I'm interested in the design crossover between small-scale objects and buildings, with a small idea informing something much bigger.

For me the design of furniture is an opportunity to explore and experiment with form, process and materials. It is an important part of our architectural thinking.

AROUND THE CORNER

PRECISION

GIANT'S CAUSEWAY, COUNTY ANTRIM, NORTHERN IRELAND

Formula One is a demanding sport in which innovation and extreme precision in design are constantly required. Big breakthroughs came with the development of the carbon fibre monocoque body and, later, the paddle shift electronic gear system by John Barnard. When Lewis Hamilton won his first world championship, his success was greatly assisted by innovations from Doug McKiernan, McLaren's chief aerodynamicist.

Doug McKiernan: I guess what we did in 2008 was to evolve the car at a rate faster than our competitors; in that year we pretty much reached the peak of F1 aerodynamic design. We spent our time trying to tailor the aerodynamics according to feedback from the drivers out on the track – if we could give them what they wanted, they would have more confidence in the car and drive the better for it.

The 2008 model had a very novel diffuser design – the diffuser is the ski-ramp-looking object that rises out of the back of the car. Regulations define its height, and the height dictates its overall downforce, which helps the car to grip the road, especially important for fast cornering. We worked round the regulations by making the diffuser part of the rear suspension. We increased its height but could claim that it wasn't a diffuser, it was part of the rear suspension – a cunning plan. The other teams picked up on it pretty quickly; it was the biggest aerodynamic development in years. And we were very aggressive with the front and rear wing design. We had an upgrade every two or three races on the front wing – all iterations towards the perfect execution.

Each development was little more than a subtle refinement, but they can make microseconds of difference over a race, and races are won by microseconds. Aerodynamic design in F1 is not so much about different overall shapes any more, it's more about understanding how to manipulate the "buoyancy fields" around the car and then make adjustments for low pressure here, high pressure there. We had to really understand the CFD (Computational Fluid Dynamics), using algorithms to solve complex airflow problems. It was that sort of attention to detail which gave us the constant level of upgrades. We spent a lot of time in the wind-tunnels, checking the cars, putting them out on the track and bringing them back in again to repeat the process. McLaren went as far as that set of regulations would permit, and we won the aerodynamic race. To come out on top last year was fantastic.

What do I think about the new, tighter rules? I think they're absolutely brilliant! Regulation encourages innovation. It is a clean sheet of paper; we've all been busy trying to answer the question, "How are we going to make this work?" Now that all the winglets and flick-ups and deflectors have been banned, the cars look a lot slicker.

MCLAREN F1

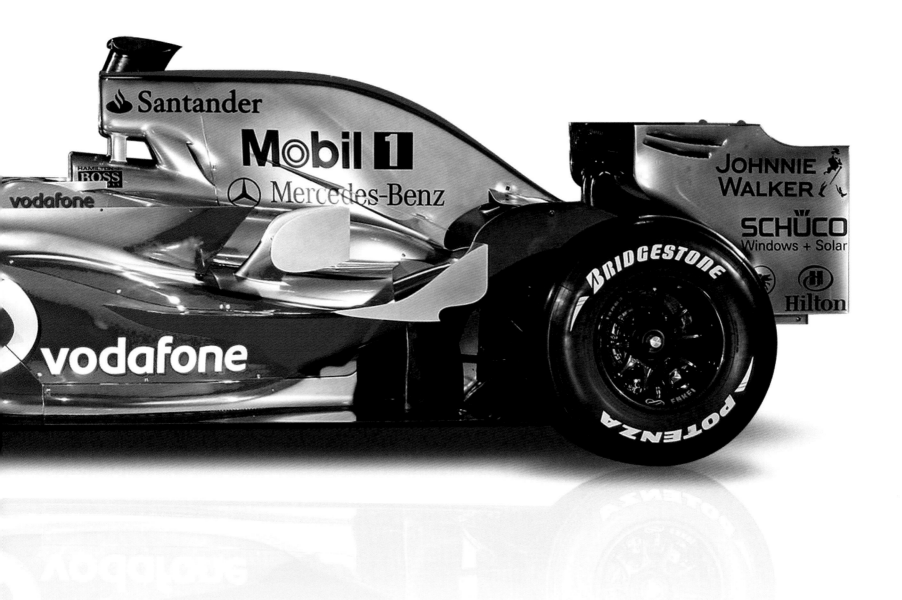

Some students make an impact in their graduation show. Rowan Mersh sold two of his pieces to the V&A, sold another to a private collector and won an art award for a fourth. Not bad for a first show consisting of five pieces...

Rowan Mersh:
I studied Multi-Media Textiles (BA) at Loughborough before going to the Royal College of Art. By my final year, I must confess, I was a bit fed up with the textile industry. So many students do great work but can't put their own name to it; their designs get sold off to fashion houses.

I started developing sculptural elements to my work, and, by my final show in the summer of 2005, I had made a series of five textile sculptures based on an examination of my environment; on what makes me who I am. *The Shape of Music* is made from CDs and vinyls from my own collection; I've put them inside pleats of striped, stretched, knitted jersey. The pleats act like stretchy tubes and can hold the discs in place without any need for an internal framework.

The piece is modelled as a dress, but of course, it's more sculpture than practical clothing. Part of the way I work is to photograph objects on the female form, which becomes an architectural environment, a static space. Each time *The Shape of Music* is shown, it's exhibited in a different way: for example, hanging between two walls. It all packs down into about a foot in diameter, and it moves beautifully as you open it up.

It's the purity of form that appeals to me, the geometric landscape. The piece relies on the fabric's inherent qualities and I've tried to use the fabric to the limits of its capabilities. I made it as simply as possible according to an almost mathematical pattern: I had to measure the length and width of the stretch and calculate the lengths of the tubes. The knitting stripes were really important for accentuating the form; a printed stripe wouldn't have worked so well; the stripes would have "bled" slightly and wouldn't have made perfectly straight lines... It won the Mercury Prize Art Competition.

I sold another piece from the collection to the V&A. It was the *Big Ball* piece, a 2.5metre-long fabric sculpture with 900 balls contained in tubes of fabric. Each ball was signed by people from the RCA, so, in a way, it summed up my experience at the college. Another contains coins collected from my travels around Europe. For the last three years I've been working as a sculptor; I have a small jewellery label, which I plan to show in an exhibition in Paris in March 2010. I now work a lot with curators and on private commissions plus other client-based projects. At the moment I'm giving textiles a bit of a break...

THE SHAPE OF MUSIC

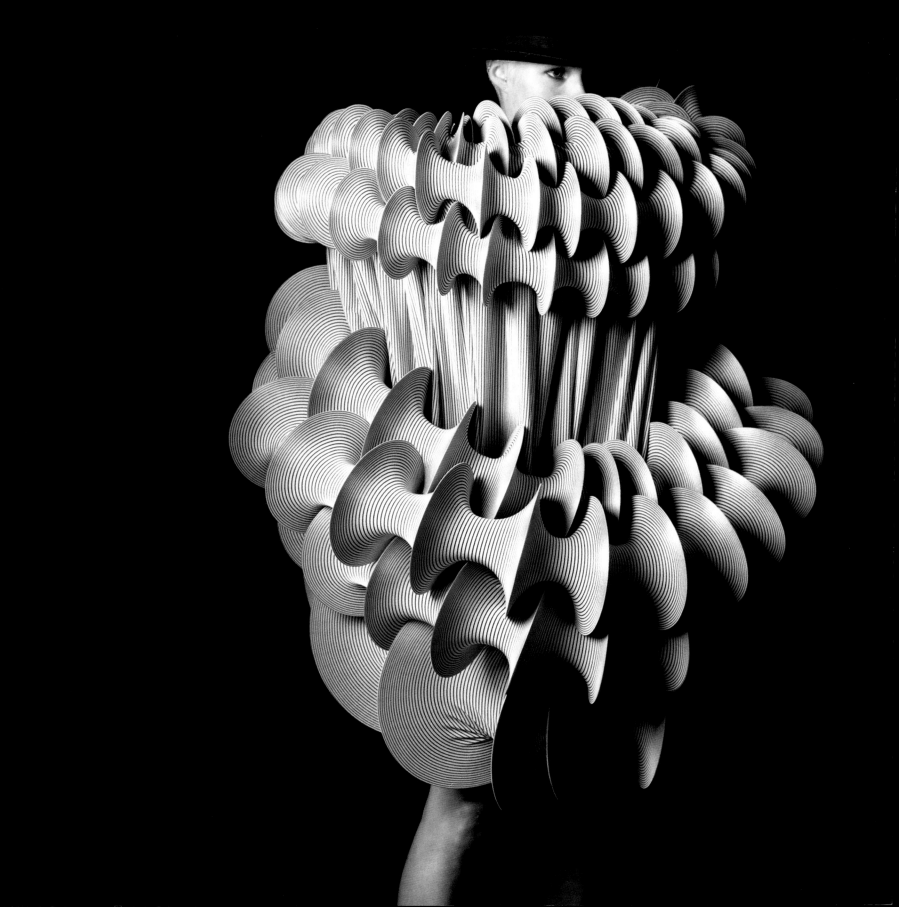

The Millau Viaduct has been described as one of the most beautiful bridges in the world. The bridge connects the motorway networks of France and Spain, opening up a direct route from Paris to Barcelona. It was designed by Foster + Partners.

Norman Foster:
The Millau Viaduct crosses a small river in a gorge between two plateaux. Based on how you read the topography, there were two ways you could approach the design. You might say that there was a case for making a big span over the river because the river is the historic generator of the landscape. And that leads you to a very recognisable engineering solution. Or you could say that the idea of spanning the river is a nonsense, since it is now so narrow that you can almost jump across it. We saw that the question was not about the river at all. Rather, it was how to span from one plateau to another in the most elegant, and economical manner. The solution flowed from that basic standpoint.

The design was a creative fusion between architecture and engineering. Working with Michel Virlogeux was essentially a meeting of minds – there was a shared passion for the poetic dimension of engineering. We made many models that we reviewed together with colleagues in the London studio. We introduced numerous subtle refinements. For example, we chamfered the vertical columns to lighten them visually, we introduced the curve on plan so that the verticals would never visually overlap for the driver, and we shaped and refined the parapet and explored different detailed options. Interestingly, there was never a conflict between what the structure wanted to be and the aesthetic ideas, at any point along the way.

The idea that you can build over a distance of 2.5 kilometres, peaking at the height of the Eiffel Tower, is, to me, absolutely astonishing. Just as a technical feat it is quite amazing.

There were a lot of detail challenges because the wind-forces at this level are incredible and the columns have to accommodate the enormous expansion and contraction of the concrete deck. Each column therefore splits into two thinner and more flexible columns below the roadway, forming an A-frame above deck level.

The columns are cable-stayed, and the cables form a fan arrangement between the carriageways. It is very elegant, very taut, and creates a dramatic silhouette against the sky. But crucially it makes the minimum intervention in the landscape.

If it is beautiful it's because its logic has been developed to the point of absolute refinement. The visual delicacy of the end result reflects a shared intent to create the most discreet intervention in the landscape. There was a structural discipline to that, of course – you might describe it as doing the most with the least – but there was also an aesthetic component. To give one example, the cables tend to recede against the sky because they are painted white. If we had painted them a dark colour, the reverse would have been true. If they had been dark they would have receded when seen against the landscape – an appropriate solution if the structure was to be mostly viewed in that context, which it is not.

A bridge is about communication in the widest sense, not just between cities or plateaux but also between people. If a bridge can also inspire the people who cross it, then so much the better – in that sense, it also becomes a symbol of place. I am told that many people drive along the motorway just to cross and admire the beauty of the bridge for its own sake. In that sense it has become a destination in its own right and also delivered a much-needed boost to the prosperity of the region.

THE MILLAU VIADUCT

Shaun Leane has taken a classic idea for wedding jewellery and given it a contemporary twist. His beautiful work is a symbol of the marriage union.

Shaun Leane:
I wanted to go into fashion after school, but was too young to attend a fashion college. My careers officer found a jewellery foundation course that I could attend at 16, so I went there to bide my time until I could fulfil my dream. But as soon as I made my first piece, I fell in love with jewellery; I realised that I had created something that was substantial yet delicate, that would be around for a long time... I was hooked!

I did an eight-year apprenticeship and was classically trained in Hatton Garden in London, working for Asprey and Garrard, making coronet clusters and tiaras. Thirteen years after my apprenticeship began, I started to design. I then began working with Alexander McQueen, making jewellery for the catwalk. His fashion had a powerful influence on me: I could use a traditional style and fuse it with avant-garde concepts; I could make something classic with a contemporary edge.

I soon developed my signature style, using tusk shapes to create jewellery that was elegant, refined and strong. The Entwined Ring Set came from my desire to do something more romantic with engagement and wedding rings, something that was aesthetically different from what was on the market. Most people buy a diamond solitaire engagement ring and then put a wedding band next to it. I wanted to create a set that looked like they were made for each other; that symbolised the romance of marriage.

The engagement ring uses the classic solitaire diamond held between two elegant arms that interlock with the wedding band. The idea was that the two rings, when put together, looked like one object, with the wedding band wrapped round the engagement ring. The wedding band is pavé set, with the diamonds in small holes set almost flush with the surface. The engagement ring is polished smooth, providing a contrast, making an exciting project and a matching contrast. You can, of course, buy them separately; at first people don't realise they're separate, and are surprised when you take it off and they see that it's made up of two rings.

ENTWINED

Rolls-Royce was commissioned to develop the engines for the new Boeing 787 Dreamliner. Made mainly from composite materials, the aircraft is setting new standards in fuel-efficiency, comfort and reliability. To achieve this, as Rolls-Royce chief engineer Andy Geer realised, a new approach to jet engine design would be required. The result was the Trent 1000.

Andy Geer: Our brief was to produce a jet engine 15 per cent more efficient than those on previous mid-sized aeroplanes, with all the environmental and running-cost benefits that would bring. It had to be more fuel-efficient across a wider mission range, for both short-haul flights and long ocean crossings.

It was a mixture of innovation and evolution, a honing of knowledge we had already developed. The main innovation was to adopt a more electrical configuration: instead of providing high-pressure air to drive on-board systems, each engine generates electrical power to the tune of half a megawatt. To achieve that we had to change the standard engine architecture. Rolls-Royce large turbofan jet engines are split into three sections, low, intermediate and high pressure. Usually, power for the aircraft systems is taken from the high-pressure shaft. But, to accommodate the varying demands of the electrical systems, we designed the Trent 1000 so it could take the power from the gear drives on the intermediate shaft. By doing this the engine can run at higher efficiency and lower idle speeds, which contributes to low fuel-burn, especially in descent. But would the system allow us to start the engines reliably? We expected to have to link the intermediate- and high-pressure systems so they could work together to ensure easy engine start, but by good engineering we were able to eliminate the shaft-linking mechanism and still achieve good performance with reduced weight and complexity.

One key innovation was to change the manufacturing process of the turbine blades so we could put more sophisticated shapes on the inside of the cast blade. We needed to do this because the temperature around the blades is high enough to melt the metal that they're made from. Normally they are cooled with high-pressure air, but the redesign allowed us to use a lower volume of the same pressure, which is far more energy-efficient.

Other innovations include the low-speed, titanium, swept fan blades in the front of the engine: they're the quietest and most efficient fan blade design in the world. We also introduced "intelligent" Engine Health Monitoring, in which enhanced sensors provide faster fault diagnosis. This means the pilot knows of potential problems much earlier, and the constant monitoring means higher reliability, lower disruption and better operational flexibility. The result is the most efficient jet engine on the market. We're now working on the daughter engine, the Trent XWB, for which there are even higher efficiency targets.

ROLLS-ROYCE TRENT 1000 ENGINE

Established & Sons encouraged furniture designer Terence Woodgate to work with the Formula One design guru John Barnard to produce a piece of furniture at the cutting edge.

Terence Woodgate: I was helping out with talks at the RSA and suggested that fashion and engineering might make an unusual combination – they rarely get to talk together on stage. One thing they have in common is the "tailoring" of fabrics, so I contacted John Barnard, famous for his amazing carbon fibre innovation in F1, and went down to his factory, B3, in Guildford. I returned to Established and ranted to Tamara and Mark about how jealous I was of the materials he worked with – titanium, magnesium, carbon fibre – you rarely get those in furniture design. They suggested that we collaborate.

It all happened in a very English way; there was no brief; John and I just sat down over a cup of tea and said, "OK, what do we want to do?" We decided upon a large table that was as light and thin as possible: a leaf of material stretched between four legs.

John Barnard: The wafer-thin table was Terence's concept; it was up to me to make it possible. To test oscillation, we made a 2.5-metre tabletop prototype from a foam core with a steel shell. If you bumped into one end, it would shiver on the thin legs for quite a while, which would have slopped your soup into your lap. We knew that carbon fibre, which is far lighter and stronger, would cope with this much better. We now had the figures we needed to calculate how to compose the table to cancel the oscillation. Getting the legs right was particularly challenging.

The final version is 4 metres long, and it's just 2mm thick at the edges. You can stand two people in the middle and it will only bend a few millimetres. In fact you could put a Mini in the middle and it wouldn't break! It's an indulgence, but it *is* practical and they are selling. With no legs in the way it's really good to sit at, and two people can easily pick it up. We displayed a range of tables during the London Design Festival 2008, with around 40 of the UK's high fliers enjoying a meal round them.

SURFACE TABLE

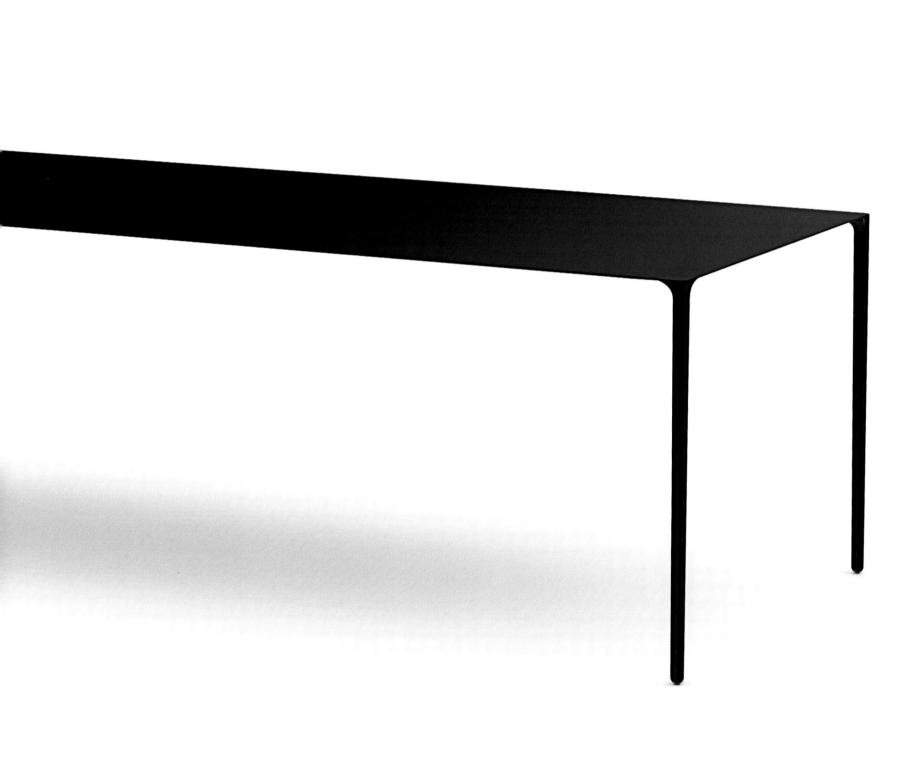

The grace and balance of Noel Stewart's hats lie in their precision. He is regularly drawn back to the Mohican style as a statement of beauty and power.

Noel Stewart: That season I was looking at an English artist called Richard Smith, and I was attracted by one of his works that features heavy blocks tumbling upwards – he managed to make cast-iron lumps move lyrically. That really appealed to me, the idea of turning something solid and heavy into something graceful.

A lot of my hats that season were inspired by Smith's sculptures; all very hard and constructivist and solid. It's often how I work; I get taken by an idea and it sort of bubbles away before filtering down. Some of the hats were about creating very large volumes around the head without looking too heavy; in fact looking chic and feminine. We made large drums covered in fabric, and carved metal shapes that would undulate around the head.

But the Cubic Mohican was more about framework than solid volumes. I have developed a habit of creating a Mohican every other season or so. For all its American Indian roots, the Mohican is a very English style. A dramatic and stunning look, it's often seen as punk and aggressive. But it has real beauty, and in this version I was looking to soften and feminise it.

We made it from ostrich quills, some bound with reflective yarn (like the whipping you use to make a fly for fishing), others made into transparent box frames.

In reality, it's very light and very stable, though I don't suppose you'll be wearing it to Sainsbury's any time soon. But it is structurally sound. Wonderfully, someone has actually bought this hat...

CUBIC MOHICAN

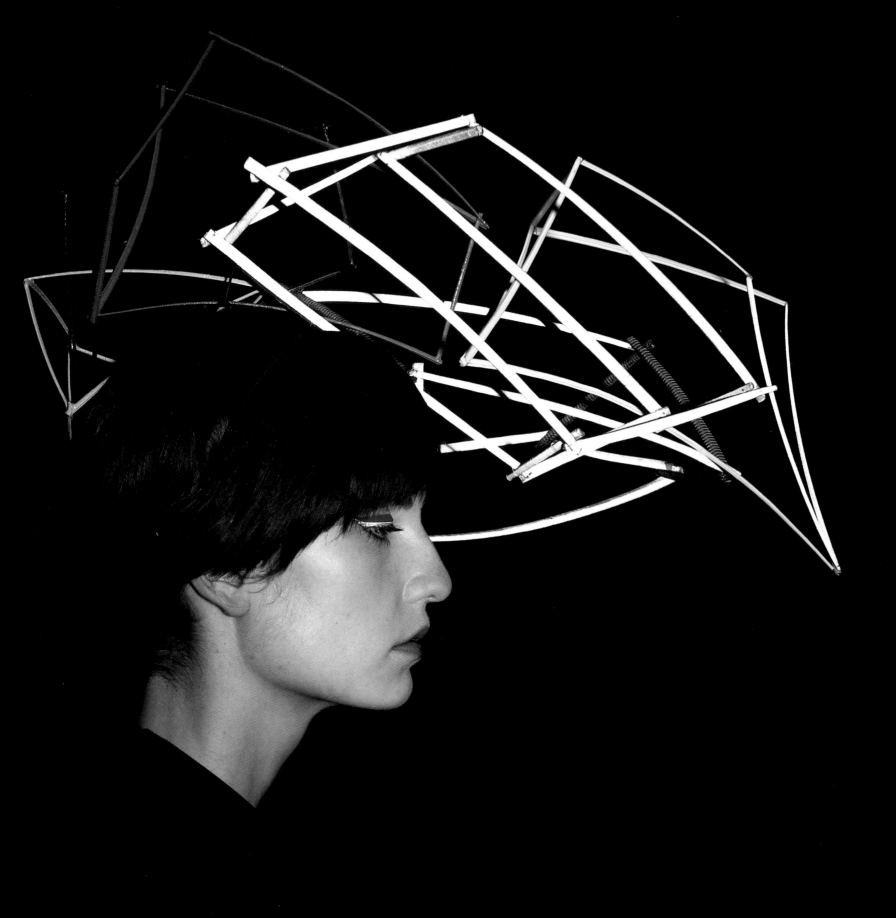

Hitch Mylius have developed an impressive reputation for high-quality contemporary upholstered furniture created with great consideration and design flair. They recently made a big impact with Simon Pengelly's hm83 seating system, and hit the spot again with the hm85 chair.

Simon Pengelly:
The hm85 project was a response to a conversation with Tristram Mylius about what he needed for the Hitch Mylius range; he wanted a generous chair that accentuated the company's unique selling point, which is all about skill and craft. This was one of those lovely projects; we'd always had an understanding and a mutual respect and we'd talked about doing something together for some time. There was a really healthy dialogue between client and designer.

We made a very conscious effort to take advantage of new technology. A standard method of making chairs is to build a timber frame, lay up slabs of foam over the frame and then upholster over that, but this method can make it difficult to create attractive curvature. So, for hm85, we used a moulded foam technique that enables you to create more organic forms and retain profiles and shapes far better, because the moulded foam can be denser and thinner than slab foam. We made a pattern by hand with polystyrene and then created a tool to cover that shape, effectively using the pattern to help create the tool. Within that tool we hung a metal frame and injected liquid foam, which expands to fill the cavity in which the frame is suspended. This enabled us to keep it looking fine and slender while still maintaining a surprising level of comfort. The method allowed us to mould springs into the seat – they're attached to the metal frame. Looking at it for the first time, you might think it would be firm and uncomfortable – but it's as comfortable as many bulkier, traditionally upholstered chairs. The slots under the arms and in the back break up the form nicely and allow the back to flex: as you lean back and push down on the arms the slots close up. It's a shape that envelops you as you sit into it; a very welcoming and inviting form.

It's an inspiration to know that however challenging your project is, Hitch Mylius will take it seriously, without saying, "Oh, we can't do that!" They will always have a go, and if they can't do it, you suspect no one else could.

Tristram Mylius:
We take a classic approach to modern furniture; we're design-led and our production methods emphasise our upholstery skills and craftsmanship. I always prefer products that combine great design with craftsmanship, comfort and simplicity. It's a fairly unusual combination.

We are constantly approached by designers who are keen to get their ideas into production. We've had a long relationship with Simon Pengelly, and, over the years, he has brought me a number of ideas to discuss. Until a few years ago, the answer tended to be, "Interesting, but no thanks...".

The relationship really got going a few years ago with the hm83, an unusual and striking public seating system. That was launched in 2004 and has had great success. Simon is immensely talented and is technically very proficient. After the triumph of hm83 we agreed to collaborate on the development of a generous and iconic armchair design, hm85.

The way it's made is of particular interest to me; foam moulded over an integral metal frame. We hadn't used that method before. It's a very relaxed armchair, extremely comfortable; it just seemed to fit the bill.

Simon and I have always had a great creative dialogue and there was quite a lot of to-ing and fro-ing to refine the design. I might say, "This needs to be bigger; don't you think this shape could be improved?" This dialogue carried on throughout the development of the product and I thoroughly enjoyed it. We've now completed hm06 with Simon, the smaller brother of hm85, and we are planning further collaboration.

Framestore was commissioned to create the bears in The Golden Compass, *an animated/live action fantasy epic that won both an Oscar and a BAFTA for Special Visual Effects. Laurent Hugueniot supervised the computer graphics.*

THE GOLDEN COMPASS ARMOURED BEARS

Laurent Hugueniot: The bears are armoured from their heads to their knees and the armour had to look metallic, rigid and heavy, with movement only at the joints. This presented the greatest challenge – how could we make the bears move realistically in their armour? We started by studying film of fights between brown bears; we even made a detailed study of a live polar bear – believe it or not, there's a company in Oxford that hires them out for the day. We studied their claws, and even inside their mouths, and noticed that their skin appears to be much bigger than their bodies, hanging from them like sacking.

We began the CG work with a simple walk-cycle to see how the armour would intersect with the bear. We then made the bears stretch and articulate to the extreme – they're among the most flexible animals on the planet! We soon found we had to cut away some of the armour and change the plates' jointing.

Armour is heavy, so, to create the impression of weight we had to use similar techniques to a mime artist, slowing down the movement to suggest muscular effort. Creating the chainmail was complex – it moves so subtly and has a sense of fall and weight. We had to programme each individual ring to move in a certain way. There were hundreds!

It was a real creative challenge to get the fur right. First we had to "groom" the bears, deciding hair length, direction, how curly, how it would vary for different parts of the body... The movement of the fur was particularly difficult, their loose skin tends to ripple as they walk, and it would have been easy to make it too stiff and tight.

The bear fight sequence was the climax of both our work and the film; it's particularly violent and shocking and I still find it visually fascinating. We were working on it almost from the beginning; the deadline was tight and it took a huge effort to meet it, but we were determined to do so while at the same time producing work of the highest quality. It was a hard, but immensely rewarding journey.

MARKS: 400 SYMBOLS AND LOGOTYPES

Pentagram's Marks: 400 Symbols and Logotypes *is a beautiful book recording some 25 years of top-quality work. Angus Hyland directed the project.*

Angus Hyland: This came about because previously we used to publish a series of "little black books" about the work we do here, each handling a different sector, like architecture, signage, packaging or identity. One of the most popular was about logos and trademarks, called, sensibly enough, *Marks.* Over the years we got rid of the little black book and, in 2007, produced one big, 800-page picture book as a giveaway, printed on thin "Bible" paper. It carries a selection of our work, in full colour throughout with full-bleed pictures — a massive tome of endless projects...

But the popularity of *Marks* prompted us to think about reformatting and expanding it. Previously it had been a collection of the previous two years' work, but Pentagram's now been around for a quarter of a century and logo and type symbols are very much at the heart of what we do. So, we thought, why not do a book that included all our partners' work since our foundation in 1972? We decided to include designs for large corporations alongside charities, small businesses and individuals.

We got all the marks we could find from the archives, some 500 of them, and laid them out on a table. We chose 400 on a number of criteria — such as whether they were famous, or graphically clever, or beautiful, or fairly represented the work across the partnership. We then put them, more or less, in alphabetical order. We decided to do all the marks in black and white because it had a unifying effect and enabled readers to concentrate more on the graphic form of each design. We added dates and a short description to each logo and used a flexy, cloth cover, complete with five place markers.

The book feels a little like a Bible; it's a similar size and has a similar muscle, with thin paper that gives you a similar "swishing" pleasure as you flick through it. This helps give it a sense of authority and offers some reverence for the content, but it's playful too. The cover's red because everything is black and white, and red is the Pentagram colour. The paper was inserted using French-fold, which means the pages have a fold

on the outside edge that you slash with a knife to reveal the printing inside. But we don't want people taking a knife to this book; the French-fold is not to save money on the print process but to prevent the black images showing through on the thin paper.

And then we threw a party for it. People told us how much they liked it and asked how they could get more, so we did a limited edition of some 1,000 with Laurence King to sell in the shops. When we designed it, we didn't plan for general publication, but we saw value in giving the public the opportunity to have a copy.

The mark I'm most attached to is probably the one for Penguin. The old mark had gradually become cannibalised and there were at least five versions of the penguin around the world, brought about by varying art departments and production techniques; Penguin thought it was high time to standardise the logo. So this was the opportunity to give the penguin a workout for contemporary audiences. Not that the public really notices, but he does a bit more work now than he did in the past. I put him on a diet, reducing his bulk by about 15 per cent (in another five years I'm going to do the same for myself). He's thinner and taller, so he appears larger on the spine of a book. I reduced his tummy and increased the thickness of the black borderline. We made the neck slash less eccentric and accentuated the gap between his flippers and the tummy. We reworked his feet to sit on a horizontal line and tilted his head up by about two to three degrees to make him more chipper.

Sainsbury's Skincare 2006
Range of beauty products for a UK
supermarket chain

Saks Fifth Avenue 2007
Iconic New York retailer

Asea Brown Boveri 1987
Multinational engineering company with operations
in over 100 countries

Asia Society 1991
Dedicated to fostering an understanding of and
communication between Americans and the
peoples of the Asia-Pacific region

Fine Line Features 1991
Film production company

Tesco Finest 1998
Premium range of food and drink for Tesco

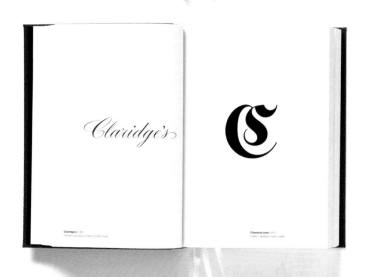

Claridge's 1991
Identity for the London luxury hotel

Classical.com 2001
Iconic classical music retailer

Biba 1960
A love-beads fashion boutique

BitStreams 2000
Exhibition of digital artwork held at the
Whitney Museum of American Art

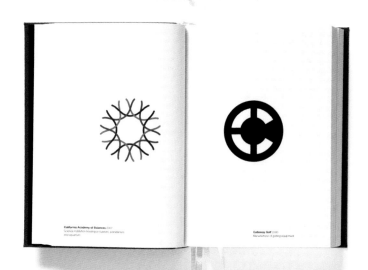

California Academy of Sciences 2001
Science institution housing a museum, planetarium
and aquarium

Callaway Golf 2006
Manufacturer of golfing equipment

Scott Drawer is the head of research and innovation at UK Sport, the government- and National Lottery-funded agency charged with delivering British success at the Olympic and Paralympic Games. The results of his work were impressive in Beijing, where Britain won a record number of medals and laid the foundations for the future.

Scott Drawer:
For any research and innovation project to have an impact, it must be a collective effort – it can't work on its own. For the Olympics and Paralympics, you need naturally talented, committed athletes supported by quality coaches, technical experts, first-class medical backup and access to the right facilities at the right time. Once you achieve all that, then it becomes possible to deliver success.

Our role has been innovation and design management, bringing together the best experts from industry and academia and forming them into small "commando units" tasked with delivering solutions within the time scales. We have a mix of people from within the specific sports as well as from a wide range of disciplines outside; experts in engineering, textiles, mathematics, neuroscience and physiology. And we selected people who wanted to take part for the right reasons, who understood that it's all about supporting the athletes and helping them to maximise their performance.

In track cycling we knew we had a wealth of athletic and coaching talent, but so did other countries. The key performance challenge was to understand and reduce aerodynamic resistance and drag. So we had bike designers, computation specialists, experimental scientists, aerodynamicists from Formula One and experts in materials all working together at the High Performance Unit to refine and develop their methods so that we could understand the problems and bring new concepts and ideas to the table. We investigated a huge number of components that covered everything from the helmet and the garment to the bike itself. We used wind-tunnels to give real-time visual feedback and optimise the cyclists' positions on the bikes. All that worked to give our riders a technological edge; there was no one component that made the difference – it was all about clever integration. I can't give you the details of any of these innovations; that's why we scrapped all the bikes from 2008 – we don't want the ideas copied! Now we're investigating new and innovative concepts and increasing our understanding through better methods.

We also had medical- and human-science experts who worked to improve the athletes' performance, as far, of course, as the rules allowed. They helped work out the best ways to train, eat, drink, rest, recover, manage jet lag and prepare for a thermally stressful environment, and they came up with clever ways to reduce and treat injuries and accelerate recovery.

Each sport is different, and there's plenty of scope to be creative and gain advantage, so it was vital to generate the right creative environment. People were encouraged to come up with ideas; they knew they would not get shot down or be embarrassed for suggesting something new or extraordinary. But they also knew that they had to deliver as quickly as possible; four years is not a long time. The real trick was finding the right people who were passionate about our success and open-minded enough to be questioned about their own expertise. Had they all had their own agendas and egos, we would never have got there.

When we started this programme it was an 8–12-year plan. The system began to deliver success in Beijing in 2008. Since then we've been busy analysing what worked and what didn't. Gradually we are adding even better quality people and trying to hit the accelerator to get it all done in time for 2012. If you get the best people and can ensure that the relationships between them are working, it then becomes a question of letting it grow and evolve.

TEAM GB INNOVATION

TRANSPARENCY

OXWICH BAY, SWANSEA, WALES

The Senedd (Senate) building of the National Assembly for Wales, in Cardiff Bay, has won awards for its environmental credentials. But the factor that really drove the design by Rogers Stirk Harbour + Partners was the idea of making the democratic process transparent.

Richard Rogers:
From the beginning we aimed to put the workings of democracy clearly on display by making the building as transparent and accessible as possible. We designed a large roof to stretch out beyond the glass walls, offering shelter to the public both inside and out. Below, a slate floor starts close to the water's edge and flows up through the whole building, inviting people in. For the inside we wanted to create a "living-room for Wales". You'll see people looking at the view, eating sandwiches in the upper-level café, or peering down through glass panels into the assembly itself, watching the politicians at work in the debating chamber below. A wood-clad hood hovers over the assembly, both marking the importance of the debating chamber and playing a key part in the circulation of fresh air. Sustainability was a vital part of the design, and the renewable energy systems should mean that running costs are up to 70 per cent less than a typical office building.

Ivan Harbour:
The original site was rather grim – a business park on the newly regenerated Cardiff Bay – so the concept for the building came partly from the view over the water. We wanted to bring the feel of the water and sky into the building, and with it that sense of freedom.

Normally parliament buildings are split vertically into public and private domains. That can increase the sense of "us and them" – the feeling that you are not allowed beyond a particular private door. We chose to make that split horizontal, and so put the elector physically above the elected. That concept arose very quickly from our early drawings.

We've used glass as much as possible to allow the public to see into the inner workings. It's a place where you can feel that, as the voter, you are respected and the politicians are working for you.

THE SENEDD

Julia Lohmann specialises in beautiful organic lampshades. But what inspired her, and how does she make them?

Julia Lohmann:
Before I went to the Royal College of Art I spent a summer on a horse and sheep farm in Iceland far away from city life. There I witnessed the whole process from lambing through slaughter to presenting the animal as food on the table. I returned to London and it struck me that, for most people, the link between livestock and food had been broken.

I wanted to make people think about it in a fresh way. I went to see a taxidermist, who taught me how to preserve animals; he gave me some of his chemicals. I was living in Tooting at the time and went to a local halal butcher to get some skins; that's where I first saw the sheep's stomachs. We once were happy to eat them but nowadays most people don't even like to think about them. I thought if I could find a way to give them beauty, I could change that. So I made the Ruminant Bloom lampshades.

As a child, you eat meat before you realise that it's part of an animal; I wanted to recreate that moment of reawakening, I wanted people to question their own reaction when they found out what the lampshades really were; people are often simultaneously both shocked and attracted. But most of us wear animal skin on our backs and on our feet without a second thought; we eat the flesh yet we get squeamish about organs. It doesn't really make a lot of sense. I'm the biggest animal lover, but I'm very pragmatic: if we eat them we should make best use of every part.

I once got a furious email from a man who had seen my website. He told me that I was awful and soulless, and what the hell did I think I was doing? The next day he emailed me again, apologising, saying he'd sent the website link to a group of friends who had pointed out to him that, had he actually read the text, he'd have understood what I was trying to do. I thought it was lovely that he came back to me.

Cows and sheep have four stomachs: the second stomach has a honeycomb texture; the other three are more "nodular". I buy the stomachs, take them home and then go through the tedious process of stripping off the meat so that only the membranes are left. I put them into some preserving chemicals for a week and then hang them up to dry. They become hard and make these lovely blossom-like lampshades.

I've formed my most recent edition over balloons and other shapes so that you can get inside them to change the lightbulbs.

RUMINANT BLOOM

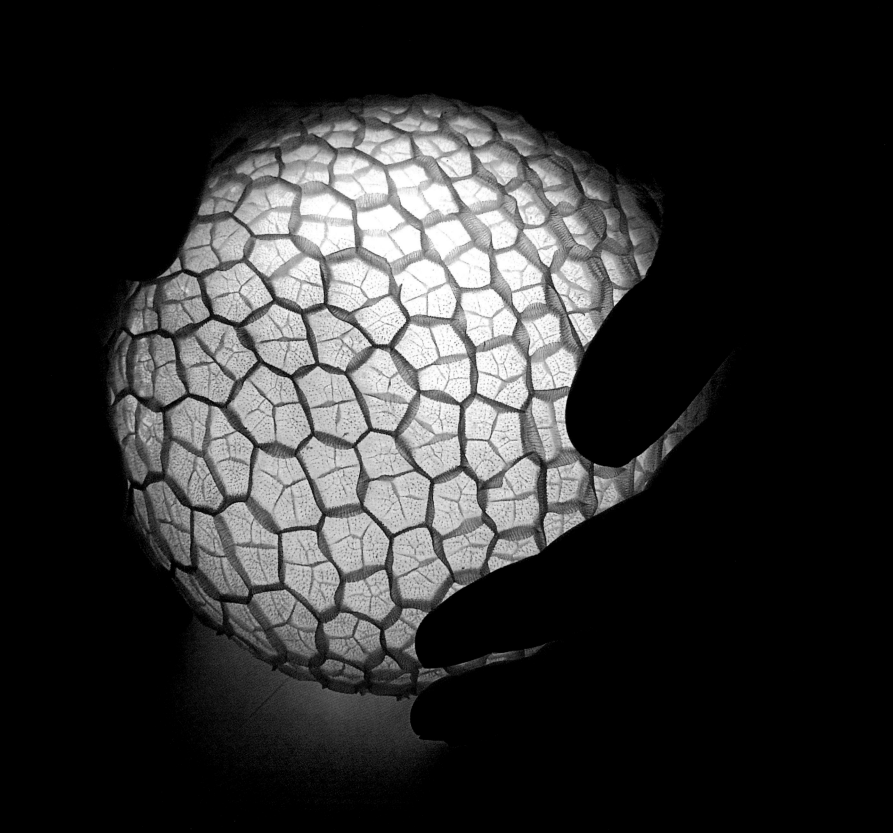

SIOBHAN DAVIES DANCE STUDIO

Dancer Siobhan Davies thought that her dance company deserved state-of-the-art facilities. So she turned to Sarah Wigglesworth to create a studio that was both practical and inspiring.

Sarah Wigglesworth: One of the special things about this project was that, by the time it was finished, we'd been working with the clients for nearly ten years, so we got to know them very well; you don't usually get that luxury. We designed three different buildings over that time. Siobhan was fed up with asking people at the top of their profession to rehearse in dreadful conditions, in unheated studios, on unsprung floors… So she applied to the Arts Council and they agreed to fund a new facility provided that she shared the studios with other dance companies.

The basic brief was to provide a warm, comfortable, inspiring space for her company and other small dance companies, a place that would be good for work and relaxation, and a space where dancers could get treatment for their aches and sprains. In the early days they were looking at something much more ambitious so we drew plans for a building including two large studios. But it became clear that the company was going to struggle to run it. They tried joining with another arts organisation but ultimately decided they needed more autonomy.

The proposed site was a constrained, robust, brick structure in London's Elephant and Castle, made up of two wings with a smaller section sandwiched in the middle. Our approach was to use the robustness of the old building as a "ground" for making quite radical changes and adding new elements that were a complete contrast. We used the curves and tensions of a dancer's body as a theme.

We opened up the central section to create a large foyer space and we put the dance studio over both the wings. As you come into the foyer you see the stairs up to the studio ahead of you. The wall on the right has been removed to give you clear views to the offices, so you know where to go straight away; all the public functions are at ground level. Overlooking the foyer at the first-floor level are the changing rooms – it's where the dancers come out after changing as they go up to the studio, so you can glimpse them in their dancewear. The first floor is a good social space for the dancers, where they can gather and chat about their day.

Siobhan was very clear about what she wanted in the studio. It had to be warm, day-lit, with a sprung floor and a 5-metre high ceiling. We presented ten different options – we knew the ribbon idea was the one she'd want. She chose it, even though financially it was a challenge. And it didn't half give us a headache! We created a billowing roof, with a view out of either end of London's skyline. It means the dancers are aware of what the weather's doing and what time it is; it's uplifting without being distracting. The studio is made out of five identical ribbons that arch over the room. At cornice height they break out and separate, twisting in three dimensions to create the billow. The underside is a curve, and, in order to get a smooth surface, we had to make the plywood panels wedge-shaped to fit the curves. They vary all across the roof. There are no sharp corners or sharp shadow and the light is spread evenly on the floor. Because Siobhan wanted to speak to the dancers without having to shout all day we had to ensure the acoustics were good, and the shape of the roof really helped with this. The whole studio was wired for sound, audiovisual screens and theatre lighting.

The rear of the building is actually in a primary school playground, so we built it as a light wall, providing something lively and stimulating for the pupils to look at. It's quite an animated façade, a patchwork of panels that control the amount of light entering the building. The staircase hangs in this space on tensioned cables. It has a sinewy feel, like a dancer holding a pose.

The Victoria & Albert Museum in London wanted to redesign the way it displayed its jewellery collection. Eva Jiricna has designed an elegant solution that itself has a jewel-like quality.

Eva Jiricna:
The brief was pretty vague. Initially the V&A wanted to find a bigger location to house their magnificent jewellery collection, sponsored by Bill and Judy Bollinger. To cut a long story short, they eventually had to stick to the original space and, in a briefing session for five different designers, they raised the possibility of adding a mezzanine floor to help display the 3,500 objects they most wanted on public view. One problem was that there weren't any accurate dimensions about space available – there was a suspended ceiling and no proper ceiling height, so there was a lot of guessing and assumptions. Since we had worked on the master plan for the building before, I suppose we were at least in a good position to guess.

After the initial analysis of our various proposals, we decided to put the mezzanine in the middle of the space. This way we could create an inviting entrance and give people an initial impression of a spacious gallery. We were also responding to fire regulations that dictated the maximum allowed distance to the exit doors. We turned the stairs into a centrepiece and designed a glass spiral staircase that itself looked like a piece of jewellery.

The decision was then taken to provide a route that would take people on a historical journey through 3,000 years of jewellery-making. One can only display objects in a narrow strip, between 0.8 and 1.9 metres off the floor, otherwise people cannot see the exhibits clearly. As a result, the display cases were built into the walls to create a continuous cabinet with no vertical partitions, allowing you to track through the whole history of jewellery in one go. The V&A wanted free-standing display cases in the middle of the room to celebrate their star pieces, so after many alternative proposals we designed two semicircular cases of variable height, which were produced by the German manufacturer Glasbau Hahn. The cases appear to be frameless and are made of double-curved glass; the star objects appear to float inside, so you can see them from all angles. It was immensely difficult to achieve.

We chose deep reds as the principal colour scheme for the shell, as a reference to a typical colour of Victorian decor; it is suggestive of sumptuous luxury and softens shadows from bright lighting. The jewellery is set on black backgrounds to further reduce shadows and the text arranged on back-lit panels – white writing on black background. It took more than a year to perfect the lighting and make it sufficiently even. Of course it has to be highly flexible so it could be adjusted for each piece.

Interactivity is an important aspect of the exhibition. There are computers installed to help visitors learn about jewellery design and manufacture. People have told me that after visiting this gallery, they feel enriched. But the security is excellent, so they don't mean financially...

Tom Stoppard's remarkable trilogy Coast of Utopia *is about a group of Russian émigrés trying to bring about a revolution in their country. Bob Crowley designed the set for* Voyage, *the first in the series. It was performed in New York at the Lincoln Center in 2006.*

Bob Crowley:
I worked on *Coast of Utopia* with director Jack O'Brien and American set designer Scott Pask. I designed the first one, which is set mainly in Russia, Scott did the second, *Shipwreck*, set mainly in Paris, and we collaborated on the third, *Salvage*, set in London.

Voyage tells the tale of a group of Russian émigrés and philosophers who all have to get out of Russia because of their beliefs: they wanted to free the serfs. The trilogy has a sweeping, epic, European canvas and includes several revolutions. We had to put Russia on stage, which is quite a thing. I was inspired by an exhibition of Russian paintings that I'd seen at the Guggenheim the year before; fantastic – grand landscapes full of romance, the reality behind which, of course, was the fact that the system was supported on the backs of millions of slaves.

I created ripped gauzes as backdrops to suggest the vast skyscapes and landscapes of the Russian plains. Gauze fabric is an established theatre designer's device; if you paint it on the front it can make a solid-looking image, but if you light it from behind it becomes transparent. It has a liquid, painterly quality; it's quite a magical thing to put on stage. I also designed a black mirrored floor to create a reflective, double imagery. The opening images in the script featured hundreds of serfs; we couldn't afford to have hundreds of actors, so I made dummies and lined them up on stage.

There's a moment when the landowner is waxing lyrical about the beauty of the Russian landscape, while the audience sees in the background this sorry train of peasants around a loaded haywain. They're toiling away to provide him with the opportunity to sit in luxury in his courtyard quaffing wine and philosophising. During the play you begin to understand the inevitability of the Russian Revolution. Another powerful image from the play was the massive ice sculpture of St Basil's Cathedral in Red Square. Actors skated beneath it on what looked like black ice. That's the image that still stays with me.

The most difficult aspect of the trilogy is that it's designed to be performed in a single day – nine hours of drama. If you're doing a one-off play, it's not so difficult, but changing the scenery for three plays performed back-to-back creates some major design and logistics problems. The plays weren't always done together, but when they were, on Trilogy days, they sold out. It was a major event and people were queuing round the block; they came with picnics and, over the course of the day, struck up new friendships.

I think stage design works best when it has metaphorical weight. I'm not interested in reproducing filmic reality on stage – I leave that to TV and film studios. Good theatre requires an imaginative leap from both the audience and the actors; it's a two-way street.

COAST OF UTOPIA

British Airways wanted something that defined Britishness in a modern vernacular for their First Class lounge at Heathrow's new Terminal 5, and invited Christopher Pearson to see the new space. He proposed William Morris-style floral prints set in 3D laser glass etchings, each with a special twist.

Christopher Pearson: BA gave me the floor plans to the T5 lounge and asked me to pitch some ideas. They were very interested in modernising Britishness – taking our fame for design and craft history and moving it into the 21st century.

I got the etched glass screen idea from a tourist souvenir I picked up in Barcelona; it was the cathedral etched into a tiny square of glass. I found it absolutely fascinating; it looked like it must have taken months to do it! I thought – could we do something better than this?

So I contacted laser-etching experts Vitrics in France, and was put in touch with Jeremy Buckland. He had the biggest machine in Europe for making laser etchings, and was capable of doing sheets of glass one metre square. I wanted screens that were 3.5 by 2.5 metres! So we started looking at ways to enlarge the machine's capacity. I also spent time working with designers at Squint/Opera to make up the 3D models.

Etching technology is pretty amazing. You fire two lasers into the glass and, at the point where the beams meet inside, they heat up the glass until it shatters. It looks like it's been scored by hand. It allows you to "draw" inside the glass. It was a very complicated project; every time we thought we'd nailed it, there was always another problem.

In each screen there are six "irregularities". There might not be a devil in the detail, but there are spiders' webs and bowler hats. Peer into the screen and you might find a veined leaf that, on closer inspection, turns out to be a winged fairy spreading her magic dust, or a roadmap of the British Isles, or a butterfly… all irreverent and eccentric British humour…

I'm a lover of immense detail; I wanted people to really enjoy the amount of work inside the screens. I also wanted to get the most out of the William Morris floral designs, trying to develop them as he would have. It's all about the accessibility and how people enjoy it. The screens have completely taken over the room – which was not the intention at all. But I'm pleased that people find them inspiring.

OAK SEASONS

Terminal 5 is an architectural triumph, not least because the design had to evolve in step with an industry undergoing a revolution. Mike Davies of Rogers Stirk Harbour + Partners (formerly Richard Rogers Partnership) was involved in T5 throughout the two decades of this £4.3 billion project, including the last eight years as project director.

Mike Davies: Tenacity: that's the word that sums up the T5 experience. Nineteen years is a long time for any design and construction process. The project was subjected to the longest enquiry in UK history – longer even than Sellafield. We developed four design concepts in that time. The first was the Flying Carpet; a scheme which featured a wavy roof, itself a symbol of flight, light and air, which adopted Stansted Airport's brilliantly radical approach of putting everything on one floor, with all the technical support systems in the basement. The Flying Carpet design was based on BAA's original T5 site, which stretched to the M25. However, objections regarding green-belt issues and the scale of the project meant we had to retreat to the boundaries of land already owned by BAA inside the airport perimeter.

As a result of the compressed footprint we went from a horizontally spread concept to a compact skyscraper that we called the Canyon Scheme. It featured three main process areas, or "plates" (Check-in, Security/Processing and Air-side) separated by "canyons" that brought light down to the lower floors. We wanted to improve conditions for incoming passengers, who normally have a poorer travel experience because they spend less time in the building than departing passengers. (We developed this concept further with Terminal 4 at Barajas Airport, Madrid.)

Then things changed again. The industry was growing at about 8 per cent a year. Retail increased dramatically, earning more for the airport than the planes themselves. Airlines wanted to give incoming and transit passengers better welcome, reception and eating facilities. Following the Lockerbie bombing in 1989, security started its massive ramp-up. The "three plates" concept became suspect – what do you do if one of the plates has to expand dramatically? The new buzzwords were "flexibility" and "loose-fit".

So we moved away from the "plates" concept and even decided that roof-supporting columns were an issue – they always seem to land up in the wrong place. At Stansted the retail is jammed against the structure; the two are uncomfortable together. Our third approach was the Tied Arch, a longer span with a steel tie that ran through the building to stop the walls being pushed out by the weight of the roof. But we found that even the 800-ton, floor-level tension tie was a constraint.

And so, finally, we progressed to the Free Span concept – a loose-fit external envelope that's entirely independent of the interior; a permanent carcass with a fully flexible inside that won't require major planning applications in the future. In some ways it was a return to the Pompidou Centre, where the building provides as little constraint as possible to the exhibits and ever-changing contents.

At T5, unusually, the wall structure is part of the roof structure and is formed by the 700-ton tensioned tie-downs that hold the roof in the air. These tie-downs are glazed, creating 27-metre high, 400-metre long, transparent façades. The roof, 170 metres wide and 400 metres long, is a visual delight! Light and airy, it floats effortlessly over the space – the biggest single public space in the UK. It makes me feel good, I smile every time I go through T5!

"Light, air and view" are the three things passengers always ask for. The Free Span concept responds to these needs, providing a calm passenger experience, using tension to take away the tension. It's big and generous yet does more with less.

HEATHROW TERMINAL 5

Christopher Kane made a dramatic impact on the world of fashion with his Spring 2009 collection, for which he created couture of distinctive originality with a series of clothes featuring scallop shapes.

Christopher Kane: I was brought up in a dull and grey town just outside of Glasgow. I've always loved art and whenever I saw fashion shows on TV I was amazed by the colour and by the dramatic sexuality of the women — it was just so opposite to how I lived. It was a world I wanted to be a part of.

I work a lot with my sister, Tammy. When we're putting a show together, we don't start with images in our mind — we start from the opposite direction. We play with fabrics and drawing. We'll often pick something that's deliberately not about fashion; it might even be ugly. But as you play around with this stuff, you get inspired. And then, along the way, TV and films have an influence, making you aware of a mood that you might want to create. This usually happens just a couple of weeks before the show. I wish it happened earlier, because that would make life easier, but you know how it is: you go to bed loving an idea and wake up the following morning just hating it. Sometimes we make major changes just hours before the show begins. We might be fitting the models, and suddenly we'll see a completely new direction. It's the most exciting part, that rush towards getting it right for the show.

The scallop idea came out of my love for big textures and fabrics. At the time I was looking at films like *Planet of the Apes* and old images of dinosaurs, and wanted to come up with something that had a prehistoric feel. It was the scaly shapes that particularly interested me; the scallops developed out of playing around with different proportions for the scales. We explored their positioning all over the body, seeing how they would stand out from the shoulder line and create strong silhouettes. We did a lot of drawing — it was all a process of trial and error, really. The surprises came when we translated the drawings into fabric. We'd often be amazed by the way they moved.

I'm not doing scallops any more, but I'll probably go back to them. The designs sit there like a little treasure-chest of ideas that I can revisit when I've run out of inspiration!

SCALLOP DRESS

Daljit Singh is a designer who loves cooking. Thanks to his grandfather and a job swap he came up with an idea for a new type of gourmet sausage. To do the branding and packaging he chose The Partners, who designed a unique henna pattern on the sausages themselves.

Daljit Singh:

My grandfather was a butcher in Shimla, a hill station in northern India. He made these sausages without really realising their potential. When I was young he moved in with my parents and used to cook them up. We thought they were amazing!

I was born in London and later returned, eventually becoming creative director of Digit, a digital design agency. I have a close friend called Vivek Singh who was the head chef at the Cinnamon Club, a well-known Indian restaurant in Westminster. One day we decided to do a job swap – he had an interest in design and I was a keen cook. So he came over to Digit to be a creative director for the day and I did a day as head chef. He asked what I wanted to do and I said, "my grandad's sausages". So I did, and they proved pretty popular. It was then that it occurred to me that I could turn them into a product.

So we started thinking about a name. In the end we came up with Mr Singh's Bangras, after a type of Punjabi dancing and bangers. Moving into sausage-making is, I suppose, a bit of a departure for a designer. But in the design business you are always promoting other people's ideas and telling their stories, so it was simply about applying that knowledge to

another strand of business. The only pitfall has been that it's taken so long; when you try to do something like this on top of your day-job, things can move quite slowly…

After chatting to various people, I found a German sausage-maker in Borough Market who ran an interesting operation that seemed a good fit. The sausages are made from naturally reared Herdwick lamb and mutton from the Lake District, and feature a variety of herbs and spices for flavouring, including cardamom seeds, onion, sweet mint, fresh hot chillies, cloves, dates, apricots, dried orange peel and ginger. They're really fiery – I love them!

The next thing was to think about branding and marketing. I went for The Partners because I know them well and have a lot of respect for their work. I also thought it would be better than getting my own studio involved; we could have a more professional relationship and I could keep a little distance. They did a great job of it. As we speak, we're concluding a deal with Waitrose…

Nick Eagleton:

We'd known Daljit for a long time; we worked on the National Gallery's Grand Tour together and we both saw this as a great opportunity to do something new. So new, in fact, that last night we won best design in the packaging category at the 2009 *Design Week* awards.

It was such a perfect brief, a simple challenge around two seemingly incompatible ideas – sausages and India don't really go together. Daljit knew there was a magic idea in there somewhere and asked us to find it.

You get those briefs from time to time, pure and simple, but challenging for all their apparent simplicity.

We wanted to do something with the idea that was universally accessible, that would tell anyone who saw them anywhere that these sausages were Indian, but were gourmet products, produced by hand on a relatively small scale. So the challenge to the team was to create a brand identity that would convey the authentic Indian ingredients and make Mr Singh's Bangras stand out.

Miranda Bolter:

We came up with hundreds of ideas, mainly based around beautiful and engaging exterior packaging. But when it became clear that the sausages would be sold loose in delicatessens and restaurants, we started looking at the branding on the product itself. Straightaway that breakthrough ruled out 99 per cent of the ideas we'd had – packaging wasn't the solution to the brief.

So the question became: how do you make the sausages look special? And out of that came the idea of using henna. Each sausage has a henna pattern, specific to the flavour, which is applied directly on to the sausage using natural, edible ink. We also created a logotype and visual identity for retail packaging. The logotype has an "East meets West" personality, using Indian colours. The biggest challenge was the food safety regulations; everything that comes into contact with meat has to jump through a variety of safety hoops. We had to find the right ink to use, learn how to apply it and persuade the manufacturers to buy into the idea.

MR SINGH'S BANGRAS

Jaeger-LeCoultre recently celebrated the eightieth anniversary of the invention of the Atmos clock movement, which is so fine that it can keep itself wound merely by small temperature changes. They chose Marc Newson to create a special edition to mark the event.

Marc Newson:
Beyond creating a special anniversary edition, there wasn't much of a brief – I was really given carte blanche. It was always going to be a balance between preserving the fundamentals of the mechanism to make it work and then doing just about everything I could to give it a unique character.

The idea for putting the movement in a glass bubble came early, so, after that, it was about working backwards. The basic architecture couldn't be modified, but many of the peripheral pieces could be. I could change the dial and the hands, and then, deeper in, I started to revise the structure that holds the movement together and then modify the myriad smaller components – levers, gears, levels, screws and finishes.

I was trying on one hand to express myself through this object but also endeavouring to preserve and enhance the DNA of the Atmos product itself; it's a very particular thing – quirky and specific. So it was always foremost in my mind that the object communicated that it was clearly an Atmos clock. It was, if you will, a problem-solving exercise, like designing a bicycle.

The glass presented huge problems. The concept was a bit "ship in a bottle". Atmos clock cases are usually pretty obvious – glass doors and panels mechanically fixed together; I wanted to create a slightly more mysterious impression and make people wonder how we got the clock inside. So it's no surprise that we had a lot of difficulty doing just that!

We approached a lot of people, all of whom would have been delighted to do it, but just didn't know how to blow a rectangular glass bubble. We went to Baccarat in France, famous more for crystal cutting and fabricating, rather than glass-blowing, and were thrilled when they not only said yes but actually did a perfect job.

I'm really happy that my original proposal could be realised with complete integrity; that doesn't often happen. It was extremely satisfying!

ATMOS 561 CLOCK

MONUMENTALITY

THE LEAS, TYNE AND WEAR, ENGLAND

30 St Mary Axe, built on the site of the old Baltic Exchange, has become a new, monumental icon of modern London, symbolising creativity in British architecture. It was designed by Foster + Partners.

Norman Foster: The brief was, effectively, to reinvent the office tower. It pushed us to explore new ground structurally, environmentally and socially. The building really shows that to achieve great architecture you need a great client. Swiss Re's patronage was a spur to be bolder, to fulfil more challenging visions, to set new standards.

The building is generated by a circular plan with a radial geometry. It widens in profile as it rises and tapers towards its apex. This is a unique form that responds to the constraints of the site: it appears more slender than a rectangular block of equivalent size and the slimming of its profile towards the base maximises the public realm at ground level. Environmentally, it reduces wind deflections, helping to maintain a comfortable environment at street level, and creates external pressure differentials that we exploited to drive a system of natural ventilation.

It is also rooted in the thinking that we first explored with Buckminster Fuller in the early 1970s in the Climatroffice project. Climatroffice suggested a new rapport between nature and workspace in which the garden setting created an interior microclimate sheltered by an energy-conscious enclosure. We selected ovoid forms for their ability to enclose the maximum volume within the minimum skin – analogies might be drawn with the naturally efficient forms of birds' eggs – while conventional walls and roof were dissolved into a continuous skin of triangulated elements. With Swiss Re this same thinking generated an elongated, beehive-like form that is fully glazed around a diagonally braced structure.

The site in the City posed a number of planning constraints – such as the permitted building height and the relationship to the public realm. But the real challenges came from the dialogue with our client and their ambition to create London's first ecological tall building.

Alongside energy conservation was a concern for humanising the workplace and the way in which people communicate within a building and the way that the building, in turn, communicates with the world outside. There are many strands to our approach to all this: for example, the rotation of successive floors allows voids at the edge of each floor plate to combine in a series of spiralling atria or "sky gardens" that wind up around the perimeter of the building. Socially these green spaces help to break down the internal scale of the building, while externally they add variety and life to the façades. They also represent a key component in regulating the building's internal climate.

At the very top of the building – London's highest occupied floor – is a club room that offers a spectacular 360-degree panorama across the capital. We had to work hard to persuade our client to celebrate this space and not use it for technical plant – which is what you find at the top of most tall buildings.

Perhaps that is the thing that gives me the greatest sense of achievement. Visually, 30 St Mary Axe is bold but also quite gentle, and it's interesting how you catch glimpses of it as you travel around London. I've heard people say that it feels "friendly"; and Londoners seem to like it, which is always gratifying.

For me, the creative process is about listening, asking the right questions and understanding the needs that generate the building. It means starting with a clean sheet of paper and an open mind, and taking nothing for granted. Sometimes that process of questioning and challenging leads to new solutions, which I have characterised as "reinvention". Essentially, I believe we have a duty to design well and to design responsibly, whether it's at the scale of an airport or a door handle.

30 ST MARY AXE

Populous was commissioned to replace London's Wembley Stadium, an icon of the sporting world. It became a tale of two towers – and an arch.

Rod Sheard: The brief was simple and clear – to design an 80,000-seat stadium to accommodate football for FA, rugby, athletics and other sports. The only other element in the brief was that it had to have all of the facilities of a modern stadium. There was a desire, particularly when we started, to look hard at Wembley's famous twin towers and try to see if it was possible to retain or relocate them. But it became clear pretty quickly that it wasn't going to be possible. If you overlay the new layout on the old, the towers would pop up somewhere near Row Four of the seating, so they had to move. But estimates on the relocation costs were horrendous, and that wasn't the only problem. Such are the dimensions of the new stadium that what before looked like impressive, lofty towers would become much diminished, even stumpy. Ken Bates, the chair of Wembley National Stadium at the time, told us that he and the board were prepared to consider any changes to the brief as long as it made financial sense. That's how it became a 90,000-seat stadium. We could justify the expansion in terms of prospective ticket sales for a national arena.

The key challenge was the grass, and on that issue Ken put down a very clear marker: the grass had to be as good as, or better than, the old Wembley turf. We started looking for quantifiable information about what was needed for growing good sports grass, but were surprised to find there was precious little good data available. So we spent a year monitoring every factor that might affect the grass growing cycle: nutrients, rainfall, light, reflected light. By the end of the year we had a pretty good idea of what we needed to do. This drove the design both for the arch and the moving part of the roof; the moving roof isn't about spectator protection, it's about getting out of the way to improve the quality of the grass – some 20 per cent of the roof slides back over the southern side to open up the pitch to more direct sunlight. We learnt lessons from the Wembley data that informed our design for the moving roof on Wimbledon's Centre Court.

So the arch came out of the desire to allow the pitch to grow. What you'd normally do in a stadium is take a roof structure and distribute the load as widely as possible, but at Wembley we had a number of restrictions. We wanted to reduce shadow on the grass on the southern side, where we also had less available land to build upon. Our initial concept was for a series of four masts on the northern side that effectively held up the roof, keeping structure away from the southern aspect. Although the masts were elegant, they didn't have the presence we were looking for. We were conscious that the two towers were international symbols, and we wanted to create a new icon of great sport; the masts didn't quite cut it. So we had a design session in our Putney office with Ken Shuttleworth from Foster + Partners, in which we started sketching away, and the arch concept grew out of that. We thought that the arch would look great from inside the bowl – and, if we exaggerated it, it would look great outside too. But after applying engineering principles we quickly saw it needed to be some 300 metres high – no need for exaggeration at all. The quantity surveyor did the numbers and concluded that the arch was the best structural solution. Unlike the four masts, it only needed to touch ground twice. That meant significant savings on complex foundation work. It took about a fortnight for the computers to confirm it was the best budgetary solution; it now carries over 50 per cent of the roof load, and has worked very well as an overarching symbol of grace and power.

WEMBLEY STADIUM

Holly Cowan was in her final year at the Royal College of Art when her two-year course spectacularly came together in her final collection.

Holly Cowan:
Put simply, this collection of bags is all about fitting the human body. It struck me that handbags are often like dead weights swinging against you; I thought there should be a way to make them work better; there's an obvious logic about a bag fitting snugly into the body shape.

It evolved out of an interest in architecture and graphics but was really driven by a fascination with form and the making process. Specifically, it developed from a tailoring project in my first year that gave me an interest in the way fabric is engineered to fit the contours of the body.

I began to think that handbags could be a great expression of all of these things – the size and boldness of architecture, the clear edges of graphics, the subtle line and flow of pattern-cutting and tailoring and, of course, the satisfaction of hand-crafting.

I'd sketch a bag and then mould the shape out of foam, making adjustments and refinements with sandpaper and a knife, adding plaster or plasticine until the line and proportion were right. The process became more and more like sculpture.

The final mould for the bag's plastic shell was machine-made. The handles are patent leather and the clasp is made of wood. The idea is that, if you hang the bag on your shoulder, it should fit neatly into your waist, resting on the top of your hip.

BODY CONSCIOUS BAG

David Chipperfield Architects were commissioned to design Germany's national modern literature archive, housing original manuscripts including Franz Kafka's The Trial *and Alfred Döblin's* Berlin Alexanderplatz. *The conundrum, as architect Alexander Schwarz discovered, was to prevent the museum from becoming dark and poky.*

Alexander Schwarz: The brief was to design the national German archive for literature in Marbach, midwest Germany. About 80 per cent of the 200 million manuscripts held by the museum are from the 20th century. They wanted to split the exhibition so that modern literature went into the new museum and the rest was housed in the old, with 50 per cent of the exhibits permanently displayed, the other half forming a changing exhibition. The museum also wanted to display its collection of memorabilia and personal belongings from authors, playwrights and poets.

There was a contradiction between the brief and the site. It's beautifully located on a rocky plateau next to a small park overlooking the Neckar River across a vista of vineyards, fruit trees and light industry; it's quite an interesting mix and the most attractive site in the town. But the manuscripts are fragile and have to be displayed with minimum light, which at first seemed to mean we'd have to shut out the view.

But we found a way to accommodate both the view and the stringent display requirements. The site was sloped, so we made a scenic entrance at the top and put most of the exhibits underground. You enter the building through a sort of lantern that forms the foyer. From here you go down into the exhibition rooms via a sequence of pavilion-like spaces that gradually lead you away from the daylight.

To avoid making the dark-panelled exhibition rooms uninviting, we created windowed spaces between the façade and the individual rooms, so that each time you left a room you would be in a space that offered a view outside.

So, in the end, although most of the exhibits are under artificial light, it is also a museum full of daylight. That provides relief to the visitor and establishes a relationship between the local landscape and the literature. The building was state-funded so the budget was quite tight, but the project went very smoothly with no major problems.

We found ourselves thinking hard about what architectural language to choose for a museum about language. Rather than trying to reflect modern literature, we chose calm, rational architecture with vertical and horizontal planes creating a sense of space and openness.

We used fair-faced concrete, sandblasted reconstituted stone with limestone aggregate, limestone, wood, felt and glass to lend the architecture a sensual physical presence.

The colonnade has become particularly valued by the townspeople, who like to visit the museum in the evening and promenade. People are free to walk on the roofs, which descend like terraces, and the museum has become a destination for people coming to admire the view, even if they don't go into the building itself.

MUSEUM OF MODERN LITERATURE

Magdalene Odundo's vessels are wonderful expressions of human spirituality and grace. They are reminiscent of art that has been produced around the world for millennia, yet her work feels contemporary, with each piece instantly recognisable as "an Odundo".

Magdalene Odundo: *Mutu* is an African word that sums up the essence of being human. It is my constant ambition to give my pieces a sense of humanity, to express *Umuntu* (the sense of being *Mutu*). Through this sense there is a wish to express movement, to make the work sing and dance. I try to create shapes and lines that attract people inside the pieces, in the way that you might want to climb inside the heart of a person you meet, so that your knowledge of what's within might enlighten what you see on the exterior. This inner sense is so hard to express and achieve, I therefore find it difficult to talk about my own work!

My techniques are really simple and I have continued to try to develop methods that are appropriate for what I make. My vessels are all hand-built and I use a combination of methods. Sometimes I lay the clay in coils around the walls of the structure, pinching, pulling and stretching it to thin the walls and form the shape; it's a method that is actually closer to sculpting clay than to coiling. I use ribs and tools made by myself; if I buy tools, they are usually hand-made by other artists.

Why do I do it? I have to! Every time I make a new piece I aim to learn something that will improve my experience, skill and the next work. I take simple clay and try to make simple work; it is surprisingly difficult – simplicity, for me, is a most elusive quality. Embellishing and adorning a work is much easier! To achieve simplicity using minimal tools and very simple basic techniques is a goal towards which I continually aspire. This particular vessel is 22 inches tall.

What inspires me? Everything around me; I can't really be more specific. I was born in Kenya and a great deal of my references are from traditional work in clay from around the world. Classical art and antiquity are important; drama and dance too. However, the main influence for my vessels is the human form. The body is so expansive and yet so contained; it's enormously expressive.

BLACK TERRACOTTA VESSEL

The Selfridges store in the Birmingham Bullring has become a national icon for innovative design. Future Systems broke the mould by drawing inspiration from a 15th-century Italian Baroque church to create a department store that is bold, human and strikingly 21st century.

Amanda Levete: The brief was simple: to design the best department store in the world... This gave us the opportunity to do far more than simply create another department store; we could make a contribution to the cityscape.

The site is sloping, bordered by a curving road. We saw a way to play with both the shape and the different levels on the site. So, using plasticine, we created a 3D form that responded to the particular context – that would go out to the boundaries and even project beyond. Having created this curvaceous form, we then needed to find a way to clad the building.

But we also wanted to ensure that the massive external volume had grain and a human scale. Our research led us to the Church of Gesù Nuovo in Naples, which uses the *bugnato* style (stones projecting from the walls) in a repetitive motif of carved stone, a cladding that seems to alter according to the angle from which you are looking.

We were also inspired by repetitive motifs in nature and fashion, such as the scales on a chameleon and sequins on a '60s Paco Rabanne dress. We arrived at the idea of circular discs – sometimes they look like overlapping scales, sometimes like vertical or horizontal rows. Using a circular motif had other advantages, making it easier to go round the curves, for example. The finish of the discs was critical. We looked at a variety of materials including ceramics and glass. In the end we chose polished, anodised, spun aluminium, which has great lustre and reflective qualities.

It was very important that the ambition on the outside of the building was reflected inside, but we knew that shop interiors necessarily have to keep on changing, so it was crucial to have a strong core design. We made the interior a piece of theatre, the focus of which is two sets of architectural escalators. Rather than minimising them, we celebrated the escalators with a white fibre cladding and glossy balustrades. We angled the atrium to bring sunlight into the store from the roof; Selfridges' stock moves so fast that the client concluded sunlight wouldn't be a problem. The large atrium gives a great view of the floors below.

There's much evidence to suggest that the design has changed the way local people perceive both Birmingham and themselves, and it has contributed hugely to making the Bullring among the most visited shopping centres in the world.

SELFRIDGES BIRMINGHAM

Vivienne Westwood's Autumn/Winter 06/07 show, entitled Innocent, *was full of drama, in which monumental, voluminous crinolines were joined by solemn tailoring and snappy corsetry.*

Vivienne Westwood: The show was dramatic. Girls with unruly hair and savagely red lips thundered down the catwalk, paying homage to their fore-sisters, those burnt at the stake wrongfully accused of being witches. T-shirts, skirts and leggings were emblazoned with the "Innocent" slogan and jumper dresses were decorated with Ancient Greek symbols of good luck. The idea was that we are all considered innocent merely through luck and not through any solid judicial system. It was a canvas for my political beliefs.

To highlight the witch-like qualities of the collection, I chose silks, velvets and wools dripping in devilish reds and sooty blacks. Cinched and cropped, the evening jacket became glamorous daywear, teamed with culottes and swollen calf-length skirts. The Little Black Dress had a pagan feel, with crinolines lowered to make for unusual shapes, and hoods added to eveningwear. In sharp contrast, gold sequinned jumpsuits, jackets and boots added a fiery glamour. The collection also featured tartan shorts, jackets and overcoats in nautical hues of blues, followed by mossy green tweeds. Masculine, low-crotch trousers and felt hats contrasted dramatically with the feminine drapery and nude shades of the eveningwear. Bias-cut dresses and skirts in the softest pinks and pearlised silks added a sense of the ethereal. I made ballgowns in softest floral print and red silk, with frothy skirting and streamlined sleeves, both to seduce and to remind us all of our innocence.

Much of my inspiration comes from the past; it's the only place to find ideas and originality. You can't be original by just wanting to do something; nothing comes from a vacuum. I look at paintings, clothes in museums, photographs of couture... If you can grasp what is original about a design you can use it. Imagine, for example, taking inspiration from Queen Elizabeth I. You see a painting of her that is very formalised. But things change when you imagine you are a rich person travelling along mud roads, under threat from highwaymen while on your way to see her. What would you see when you met? She would be so glittering, so white; she would look like a being from another planet.

But when it comes to making clothes inspired by this, I wouldn't interpret it like that. It's just a source, a beginning of ideas. Usually you don't see the source of my translation; it has been transformed into something else by the time I present it.

I think the real driving force behind my desire to continue working is my wish to continually surprise myself. The more I work, the freer my clothes become; the technique becomes automatic – you can practically do whatever you want by the time you get to that stage. A large influence on the collection is the natural fabrics I use – English barathea, Scottish tartan, Harris and Donegal tweed, English mohair and Swiss silk. I am also influenced by my interest in the new pattern-cutting techniques.

My clothes allow someone to be truly individual – this goes against the current thinking that says that if the clothes are nothing then the woman is important. In fact I think the opposite: if everybody is wearing the same thing, they are bound to look the same. The majority of people on the street look quite dreadful; they are lazy in their dress and take no time to express themselves through clothes. Minimalism in dress is a dominant force because people are so afraid of committing an error in taste. So my customers are the best ambassadors for my clothes. Honestly, I'm very proud of my customers.

Zaha Hadid Architects was briefed to design a Science Centre for the city of Wolfsburg, the first of its kind in Germany. Zaha came up with a remarkable design that was all about drawing the public into the Centre.

Zaha Hadid:
The site is a significant location for Wolfsburg: it forms part of a chain of culturally important buildings by Aalto, Scharoun and Schweger and is poised between the residential and manufacturing parts of the town, which are separated by a canal and train lines. It was a requirement to integrate an existing footbridge spanning the canal and connecting the city with Autostadt, a car theme-park run by Volkswagen.

The project engages with the circulation flows of its context and becomes a sort of filter for the city, as it encourages movement through the site. Multiple threads of pedestrian and vehicular circulation are pulled through an artificial landscape and into the building, creating intersecting paths of movement. The main volume, the exhibition space, is raised over an outdoor public plaza, and a new urban field has been created on the ground. The brief also called for elements such as a restaurant/bistro, a shop, an auditorium and an underground parking garage.

We had recently been exploring the idea of porosity: drawing public space into a building's interior to make a series of public rooms in a city. Porosity suggests a new kind of urbanism, composed of streams, or flows of movement, that cut through the city fabric. The building is structured in such a way that it maintains a large degree of transparency and porosity at ground level.

The ideal for Wolfsburg was to integrate the logic of access with its structural logic. The correspondent visual image was that of pulling funnels down from an elevated floor surface, so that the floors are neither piled above each other nor seen as a single volume. The elevated box is supported and structured by these funnels protruding into it and extending from it. Through some of these funnels the interior is accessible; others are used to lighten the space inside, while some of them house necessary functions. This project combines a formal and geometric complexity with structural audacity and material authenticity. A lot of time and energy was concentrated on achieving this result.

PHAENO CENTRE

Designers David Hawkins and Glenn Howard at Untitled were commissioned to mark the refurbishment of the Royal Albert Hall with a book celebrating its history using their fantastic picture archive. They asked typographer Alan Kitching to design the cover.

Alan Kitching:
David and Glenn told me that during their hunt through the archive, they came across pictures of these great billboards – things like "House Full" – all done in woodblock lettering. They thought these had the right feel for the lettering on the cover, only they didn't have any woodblock letters. So they called me.

The solution came to me when I was on the 360 bus on my way to teach at the Royal College of Art. The 360 is a very civilised way of travelling; it meanders though the London streets, giving you plenty of time to ponder. I was thinking about the Albert Hall's special qualities: its wide range of uses, its rounded shape, how it stands alone... I began to wonder how I could show that uniqueness. The bus terminates at the Albert Hall, so I went in to get a seating plan. It was then that I was reminded that the place is actually oval, not circular.

I wanted to make the type for the cover hang together like a banner, giving a feeling of celebration and carnival, and the oval curve gave me a line to hang the lettering from. I chose blue and red on a white background for obvious reasons. It's one of Britain's most prestigious venues, putting on everything from the Last Night of the Proms to boxing bouts and The Beatles. I emphasised *Albert Hall*, because that's how the people know it, rather than the grander *Royal* Albert Hall. David and Glenn liked the cover and asked me to use the same theme in the book's dividers to mark the Albert Hall's different eras.

My partner, Celia Stothard, and I bought a vast collection of wooden letters in 1997. I love using them; they're unyielding, awkward, beautiful things. And, of course, they are designed to be used horizontally, to go across the page; making them work in a curve was an enjoyable opportunity. They're obsolete technology now, of course: computer typesetting has driven them into the museums. It feels good to put them back to work again.

THE ROYAL ALBERT HALL BOOK

A VICTORIAN
MASTERPIECE
FOR THE
21ST CENTURY

Foreword by
HRH The Duke of Gloucester

THE ROYAL ALBERT HALL

PROJECTIONS

The Shanghai Expo in 2010 will see some 200 pavilions created by as many countries. So how can Britain ensure its pavilion stands out? Heatherwick Studio won the competition to design the British pavilion for the Shanghai Expo 2010.

Katerina Dionysopoulou: Expos are phenomenally busy and there's always so much competing for your attention. So, at Heatherwick Studio, we looked at people's experiences of these massive events and found that most rarely take in the masses of information – but they do remember vivid design. So we decided to create an experiential, immersive installation within and around one amazing object.

Thomas Heatherwick has been exploring the idea of a "hairy" building for some time – this seemed like a perfect opportunity to make it happen. Our first inspirations came from images of an English cornfield moving in the wind. Our site in Shanghai is near the river, so we knew we could catch the breeze. We created a 15m x 15m x 10m wooden box, penetrated with 60,000 cantilevered acrylic shafts, each 7.5 metres long and protruding 5 metres into the air outside like a blossom of hairs, or shoots and stamens. The acrylic shafts work like fibre optics, bringing thousands of points of light into the pavilion, illuminating it with an aura reminiscent of a cathedral. And it's a cathedral of seed – the pavilion itself appearing like one massive sprouting seed; at the base of each shoot, enshrined in the acrylic, sits a single seed. We worked closely with Kew Gardens' Millennium Seed Bank, which has the largest collection of seeds in the world. The seeds are the start points for the shoots that grow out of the building and blow in the wind. At night, the 60,000 shoots are illuminated, creating a spectacle on the outside.

The aim is to create a calm moment in contrast to the buzzing busyness of other pavilions. You go inside and contemplate this daylit starfield, this sprouting seedbank in the heart of a technology-dominated festival. The feeling is as if you have paused; you won't be bombarded with words or pictures; you can just have a moment to reflect as you step inside it. The pavilion is about creating that feeling of the unity of technology and nature – that sense of the two existing together.

BRITISH PAVILION WORLD EXPO SHANGHAI 2010

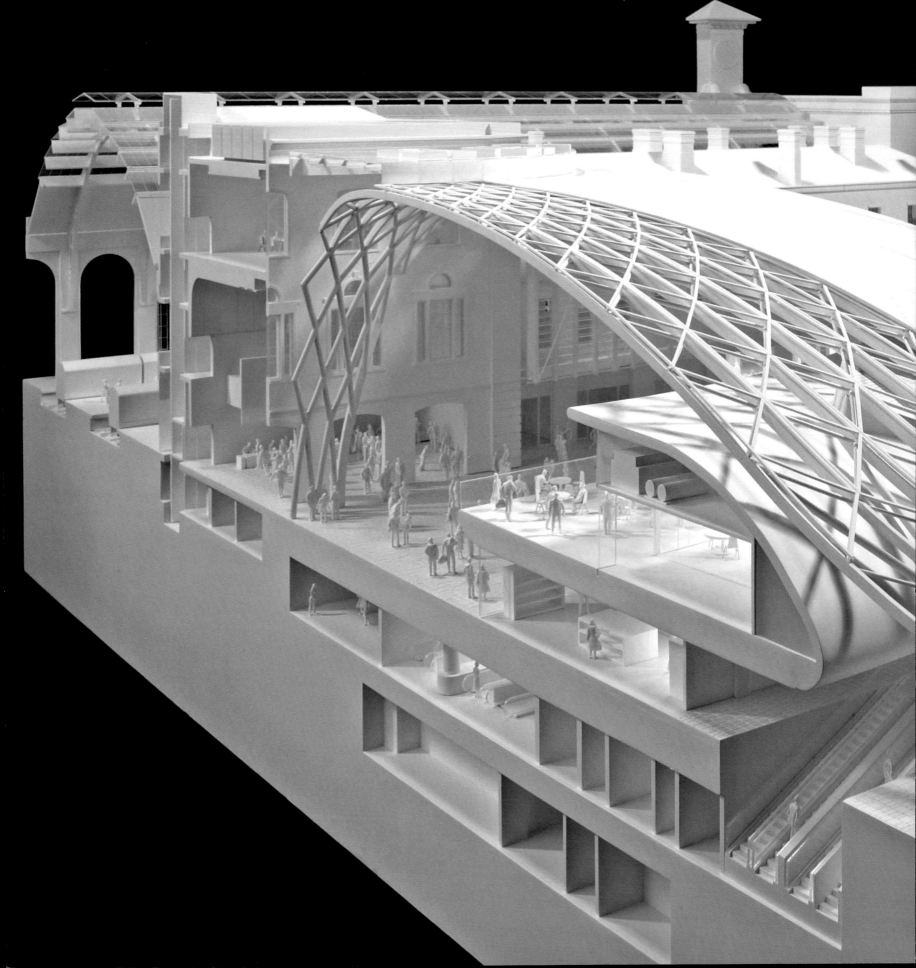

A major redesign of King's Cross Station is under way to accommodate some 50 million passengers a year – a 25 per cent increase by 2015, partly explained by the fact that the Eurostar terminal is now next door at St Pancras. The architects are John McAslan and Partners (JMP).

John McAslan:
The project began about ten years ago, when Railtrack started to look at improvements to future-proof the station. Our proposals went through various adjustments and settled down three or four years ago, when we resolved the most appropriate approach with Railtrack's replacement, Network Rail. The plan was to remove the temporary concourse from the front of the station (it had been around for some 30 years and had never been fully permissioned) and construct a new concourse to double area and capacity.

As one of the most important pieces of railway architecture in Britain, King's Cross is Grade 1 listed. But unlike St Pancras, there was no way we could fit the entire reworking into the existing train shed. A new concourse facility would have to be dramatically larger. We looked at all sorts of options, from putting the concourse inside the shed using a mezzanine, to constructing something new to the south. In the end we decided to build to the west because it's the option that works best from a connective point of view: it's right by St Pancras so it will be easy for people to connect to the Eurostar terminal and the suburban train lines. Also, the new London Underground Northern Ticket Hall is being built underneath that space, so it makes for a fast vertical connection to the tube.

The glass roof takes its form from the curve of the Great Northern Hotel, which is being refurbished as part of the site overhaul. The roof architecture springs from the centre of the 1850s ticket hall – we're going to open it up as a ticket hall once more. It is also informed by the fact that the new Underground ticket hall beneath the site has had to be built separately from this project. So we went for a long span springing like an umbrella over the concourse in a graceful sweep.

The new western concourse is just one of many elements. There will be new roads, new taxi drop-off and pick-up points and new landscaping. Phase One was the eastern range – the linear building running the length of York Way. Phase Two is the western range, including changes to the Great Northern Hotel. Phase Three is the train shed itself, Phase Four the western concourse and Phase Five the landscaping to the south and the servicing tunnels beneath the station.

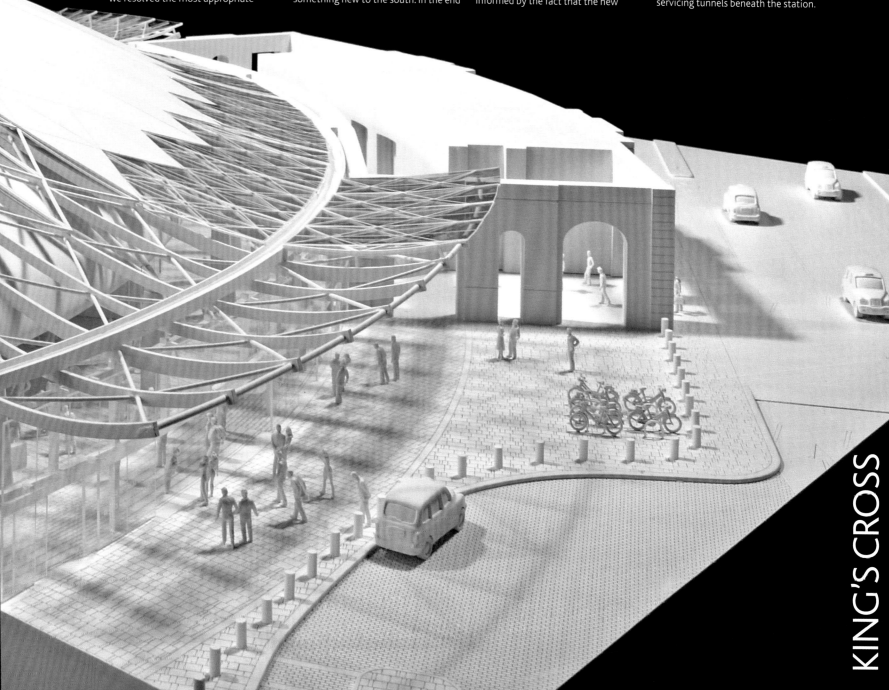

KING'S CROSS

Marks Barfield wowed the world with their design for the London Eye – so much so that they had numerous requests to repeat the magic in other major cities. Now they've designed a similar project for Brighton.

David Marks:
The idea for the i360 came from the requests from many cities around the world to repeat the success of the London Eye. We did a number of feasibility studies in places like Shanghai, New York, St Petersburg and Las Vegas. What we quickly realised was that everyone was looking at the Eye and seeing the success without really understanding the fundamentals that lay behind it. For example, in Shanghai we identified the most viable sites, but the city selected a site that didn't command any of the best views. St Petersburg offered a great view, but couldn't be sure of securing sufficient visitors to make a high-capacity attraction like the London Eye viable. You have to design an attraction for its peak capacity, taking into account seasonality. There's not much point in having a 30 per cent utilisation rate; that effectively means you've over-designed the attraction, it becomes expensive to run and would likely not be considered a success.

There are only a handful of cities that could generate the necessary visitor numbers for a London Eye-sized attraction, but many more that could provide, say, a million visitors a year. The Eye gets over 3.5 million visitors a year; its design was an innovative solution to a particular set of conditions. If you only have a million visitors instead of 3.5 million, the solution would not be a London Eye. So we started looking for a different solution.

For Brighton, the best answer was a single large pod rising up a spire, with a capacity of up to 200 visitors on a round trip of 20 minutes which could be extended in the evenings. We are working with the same team as we did on the London Eye: Hollandia (the steelwork contractor), Poma (pod and cable specialists), Jacobs, and Eleanor Harris, our commercial director. We chose Brighton because it offers amazing opportunities and conditions necessary for success, including a fantastic site. And, crucially, it's got a great view across the downs, the city and the sea. Brighton attracts 8 million visitors a year, is a well-known romantic destination and is less than an hour away from London.

As with the Eye, some people have made comparisons to a fairground attraction, but the i360 demonstrates an altogether different quality, scale and personality. At 183 metres high and 4 metres in diameter, the i360 is tall and very slender. Visitors are free to roam an 18-metre diameter pod. Hollandia has come up with a very clever way of erecting it, one that's been used before, but not for this kind of attraction. Poma has designed the systems for moving the pod up and down – the motor rooms are all at the bottom so there's easy access, and the cabling arrangement is based on tried and tested cable-car systems. It's designed to be highly energy-efficient and there is a counterweight in the middle of the steel spire. Like the London Eye it also has damping mechanisms built into the structure to avoid uncomfortable movements and stop people getting seasick.

We're aiming to open it in 2011, and look forward to seeing masses of people coming away from the experience with smiles on their faces...

i360 BRIGHTON

The Olympic Delivery Authority, along with Stratford City, the new retail, office and housing complex that will serve the Games, wanted the entire project and its legacy to be powered by green energy sources. John McAslan and Partners (JMP) was chosen to design the power stations.

Kevin Lloyd:
We were originally invited to present our initial ideas and approach in response to the briefs from the ODA and Westfield for two new energy centre buildings at King's Yard and Stratford City. JMP were then involved in developing detailed briefs for the building in conjunction with the service and plant engineers. The buildings are designed to provide electricity and hot and chilled water to be distributed throughout the sites through an underground distribution network. The power will be generated by gas turbines creating electricity and driving the chillers in the main energy plants. Hot water will be generated via a combination of gas and biomass boilers.

We carried out a study of the legacy of power buildings in London. Mostly coal-fired, these were heavy engineering-led large-scale structures. They have since become important landmarks in the city and in some cases have found future uses, for example Bankside (now Tate Modern) and the planned regeneration of Battersea Power Station. However, we were evolving a design for a new type of energy building driven by sustainable, more efficient and cleaner technology, but wanted to reflect the confidence of scale and civic authority for which the old power stations are rightly famous.

Flexibility was a key ingredient — energy technology is changing rapidly and major equipment may well have to be upgraded or replaced over the 40-year concession. So we needed to come up with a construction technique that allowed large pieces of plant to be moved through the façade. At King's Yard, the Olympic Park energy centre, the plant equipment will be arranged along the front face of the building. The plan is devised as a series of large bays on a regular grid, with each module containing at ground floor a zone for either boilers or gas engines. The absorption and electric chillers will be on the first floor.

We devised a cladding system based on using SIPS panels — a sustainable way of building up exterior skins by using a composite panel of Oriented Strand Board (OSB) made from compressed wood chippings with an insulation layer set between. Bonded to the front surface of the panels is an EPDM (ethylene propylene diene monomer) rubber weatherproof membrane. The joints between each panel are heat-welded on site. In the future, if and when plant equipment needs to be replaced, the EPDM sheet can simply be cut out. Sitting over the panelled surface on the public fronts is a semi-transparent veil of Corten steel mesh. The exhaust flues are 45 metres high and also clad in Corten steel, and are highly visible elements from within the Olympic Park.

The envelope presents a fresh approach to creating large buildings. The form of the building is an expression of the functions inside. As part of the development of the design we are planning an arts strategy linked to the concept of energy generation, using light and colour. The two energy centres will be important new landmarks, architectural gateways, if you will, on the eastern and western boundaries of the new landscape.

Zaha Hadid Architects was selected to design a venue to host the London 2012 Olympic and Paralympic swimming and diving events. She chose to express the geometry of water in her striking design.

Zaha Hadid: The Aquatics Centre plays an important role in the Games, partly because it is placed between Stratford City and the Olympic Park, so it is the first venue that visitors will approach. Within its design the Aquatics Centre addresses the main public realm spaces implicit within the Olympic Park and Stratford City planning. These are primarily the east–west connection of the Stratford City Bridge and continuation of the Olympic Park space alongside the canal.

The architectural concept is inspired by the fluid geometry of water in motion, creating spaces and a surrounding environment in sympathy with the river landscape of the Olympic Park. An undulating roof sweeps up from the ground as a wave – enclosing the pools of the Centre with its unifying gesture of fluidity, whilst also describing the volume of the swimming and diving pools. The pool hall is expressed by a large roof that arches along the same axis as the pools. Its form is generated by the sightlines for the spectators during the Games mode. Double-curvature geometry has been used to create a structure of parabolic arches that produces the unique characteristics of the roof. The roof undulates to differentiate an internal visual separation inside the pool hall between the competition pool volume and the diving pool volume.

In legacy mode, after the Games, the Aquatics Centre will be used as a pool for community use and as an athlete training facility.

AQUATICS CENTRE LONDON 2012 GAMES

Hopkins Architects was assigned the task of designing the Olympic and Paralympic Velodrome for London 2012. Mike Taylor directed the design, and his team has come up with a form that reflects the drama of track cycling and promises to be a major European venue for a wide variety of cycling events.

Mike Taylor:
The brief was for a 6,000-seat indoor velodrome with a 250-metre timber track which will become the hub for all forms of cycling after the Games; this also meant a highly sustainable building to champion the ethos of London 2012. We strove to design a building that could match the engineering of a bicycle in its efficiency. The sculptural building form captures the geometry and drama of the 7-metre wide track – a track that twists as it goes round, with banking that varies from 12 to 42 degrees of incline. The form of the upper bowl, which is clad in timber, reflects this shape as it wraps around the seating and works to keep internal volume, surface area and heat loss to a minimum.

Internally, the seating is split so that half the seats are in the arena bowl directly around the track; the other half are in the roof space. The upper tiers and the arena are separated by a ribbon of glazing, which is fully accessible from the Park, so the public can walk up to the glass and look down on to the track. It's extremely unusual for velodromes to encourage involvement in this way, but we felt this clear connection to the public realm was really important for the Olympic Park. At this glazed level there is a continuous public concourse where we have located cafés that will look both on to the track and outwards over the Park.

The roof is made from prefabricated timber cassettes, fitted over a cable net suspended from a perimeter ring beam. Like the façade, the roof panels are highly insulated. Internally they are finished in birch ply with a standing seam metal roof. It's a very efficient structure, weighing just 30kg per square metre, roughly half the weight of the Beijing Velodrome, and has rooflights that bring natural light directly into the track "infield".

We've been working closely with track designer Ron Webb and have also consulted with the GB elite squad, including Sir Chris Hoy, to ensure the track and internal conditions are ideal for major international events. By tweaking its geometry and construction details within the allowable guidelines we hope to have made a very fast, and, hopefully, a world record-breaking track.

By any country's standards, a 6,000-seat velodrome is a large venue, and this will be a great location for six-day events, helping to put London on the world map for indoor track cycling – something that's well overdue. For legacy, the interior will remain largely unaltered, as will the exterior BMX track, but the surrounding area will be remodelled after 2012 into a series of outdoor cycle circuits, including a 6.5-kilometre mountain bike course and a 1.6-kilometre road circuit for public use. This new VeloPark is set to become both a major hub for everyone interested in cycling in London and a centre for developing a new generation of gold medal winning cyclists as well.

VELODROME LONDON 2012 GAMES

HANDBALL ARENA LONDON 2012 GAMES

Make Architects were asked to design the Handball Arena for London 2012. They've come up with a building designed around the concept of flexibility that can be used after the Games by the sporting and local community for a wide variety of sports.

Ken Shuttleworth:
With the deadlines and the cost constraints front of mind, we knew this building had to be as straightforward as possible. The ethos from the outset was simplicity, efficiency and flexibility. Initial sketches were all about keeping the building simple. We went for a rectilinear form because we knew it would be easier to manipulate and adapt as the brief developed. So we avoided gymnastic structures and complex curves, going for the simplest thing we could do; it was almost a purist build. We had recently done the Judo dojo down in Dartford, the starting point for which was a judo mat. I think that work inspired the authorities to choose us.

The beauty of this design lies in its three layers: the landscaped ground layer, the glass strip and then, above, the large copper box that seems to hover over a halo of light presented by the glazing. You can enter the building halfway up through the glass strip. The copper box, which houses the upper tier of seating, will be made mainly from recycled copper. It will weather naturally, generating a range of green and purple hues on each façade. We chose copper partly because of its natural beauty and partly because it would mean that local authorities won't be saddled with high maintenance bills after 2012.

The roof is a most economical free span, with no columns except at the perimeter. We've put tubes into the ceiling to bring in natural light. This is not a Games requirement – the TV coverage requires artificial light – but we knew that, in legacy mode, the building would be more energy-efficient during the day if we could bring in as much natural light as possible. This will not only improve internal quality of space but will also help the building achieve a BREEAM Excellent rating. (The Building Research Establishment Environmental Assessment Method is the world's leading environmental assessment method for buildings.)

The building has been landscaped so that it appears from some aspects to be a natural part of the Park, which sweeps up to it from ground level. We've worked closely with the Park landscape team to embed the building in the site.

The thing I most enjoyed about this project was that we started from the inside out, generating as tight a wrap as we could to allow full functionality. It was a really nice way of doing it – there's no superfluous space and it allows it to be built quickly.

Stuart Fraser:
The brief had two distinctive modes – Games and legacy. We were asked to build a sports hall with a seating capacity for up to 7,000 to host handball and modern pentathlon fencing. It will also host Paralympic goalball, a game developed for rehabilitating injured World War II veterans, and featuring three blindfold players on either side trying to score goals using a ball with a bell inside to guide them.

We wanted the building to work as a multi-use sports venue after the Games, so that, for example, schoolchildren, the local badminton club or elite athletes could come and train, so we've also had to take into account the specific requirements for a wide variety of indoor sports. The large internal space can be divided up into areas suitable for all levels of ability. And we've designed in a retractable seating system, which folds away to increase the playing area, or folds back out to accommodate more spectators. This means it only takes a matter of hours, rather than days, to convert from a multi-use sports hall to a stadium hosting, say, European League basketball.

In an ideal world we'd have buried the building, but excavating the land on the site would have been difficult and expensive. So we chose instead to work with the surrounding topography and integrate it into the landscape to ensure that all spectators have a level access approach into the heart of the seating bowl – every spectator will enjoy the same experience regardless of any disabilities. This, for me, has been one of the big successes. The layout deals really well with high volume ingress and egress, for both Games and legacy events, whilst also being flexible enough for legacy day-to-day use. It can scale down so that only the front door is in use, making it easier to keep the building secure and requiring minimum staffing.

The Olympic Stadium in Stratford will be the centrepiece of London 2012, seating 80,000 spectators. Rod Sheard is senior principal at Populous and led the design team to build a collapsible venue.

Rod Sheard: It was a totally revolutionary brief. London 2012 had come up with the ingenious idea of creating an 80,000-seat stadium that would reduce to 25,000 seats after the Games. Olympic and Para athletic venues are often turned over to a more popular sport, like soccer, but there was no call for another large-capacity stadium in London. So we signed up to this great idea of building a collapsible stadium.

The first challenge was to get ourselves into the right mindset. Architects are brought up to build structures that will last 50 years or more; everything is focused on how you ensure it will last: that the roof won't leak, that the materials will endure the rigours of time and weather. Now we were faced with an entirely different set of parameters in which the majority of the building would only be around for a few years. We had to learn to embrace the temporary.

We soon saw how many things you can't do for a long-term building that you can for a temporary structure. Colours, for example – we didn't have to worry about them fading over time. And materials: we're making the exterior out of fabrics,

put together like interlocking banners. We've used a modular design, so we can strip out services for 55,000 spectators – such as bars, restaurants, toilets, retail, information booths and kitchens. The physical structure, including the seating bowl, is concrete and steel. That surprises some people, but the construction industry is geared up to deal with these materials efficiently, so it made economic sense. And it's all designed so you can unbolt all the elements and ship them anywhere in the world. Even the roof is detachable – you could conceivably lift it up whole and set it down in a field nearby. It's like a giant Meccano set.

We gave a lot of thought to the idea of putting in a retractable roof. But we looked at the cost against the statistics and saw that Games have never been seriously disrupted by the weather. The most important thing was to protect spectators from rain and sun. We've ensured that 60 per cent of the seats are covered, which compares well to other Games venues. The most important factor is wind – a gentle breeze can affect world record attempts. A lot of thinking has gone into controlling the wind conditions.

We've created our own aesthetic based upon the novel idea of a collapsible stadium. It's all about the sort of lightness, delicacy and clarity that a permanent building cannot have. I've really enjoyed watching those elements come out of the ground – I think the clarity is very refreshing!

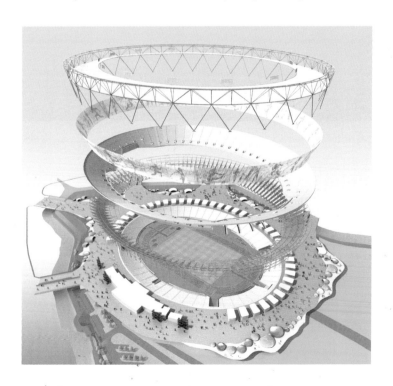

OLYMPIC STADIUM LONDON 2012 GAMES

The author and publisher would like to thank the designers and manufacturers who submitted work for inclusion and the following photographers and copyright holders for the use of their material. In all cases every effort has been made to contact the copyright holders, but should there be any errors or omissions the publishers would be pleased to insert the appropriate acknowledgement in any subsequent edition of this book.

CREDITS